Speedy
EACH DAY
A NEW DAY

W. 'Speedy' Moore

Marshall Pickering

Marshall Morgan and Scott
Marshall Pickering
3 Beggarwood Lane, Baskingstoke, Hants, RG23 7LP, UK

Copyright © 1987, W. 'Speedy' Moore
First published in 1987 by Pickering and Inglis Ltd
Part of the Marshall Pickering Holdering Group
A subsidiary of the Zondervan Corporation

ISBN 0-7208-0721-2

Text set in Plantin by Brian Robinson, Buckingham
Printed in Great Britain by Anchor Brendon Ltd, Tiptree,
Essex

Dedicated to the memory of my daughter Nina and to the Revd John Beatie, who planted the seed in my heart and to Gideons International for providing the fertiliser.

Chapter One

My Christian walk over the past decade has been a wonderful experience.

I've covered a lot of ground, met a lot of people, seen a lot of things. It's always been a habit of mine to keep a diary, and it's out of that diary, with its amusements, lessons and reflections, that this book has been born. I hope it brings to life for you some of the fascinating encounters and experiences God has given me on this 'walk' of mine.

In introducing myself it is necessary that I go briefly into my past, and I emphasise the word *briefly*, for I am enjoying my walk with God so much that I do not wish it to be marred by sordid recollections. On that lovely Sunday morning in April, 1976, He buried my sins in a Sea of Forgetfulness where all kinds of fishing are forbidden . . . hallelujah!

I was born on 30th November, 1912, the youngest of a working-class family of four. The only religion I received was during my boyhood. I was chased to Sunday School by an upright widowed mother, and sometimes attended a small back-street mission hall in my home town, Coleraine – especially when tea-parties were pending.

But on reaching that vital cross-roads in my early teen-age years I willingly followed the signpost to hell and was almost there when the good Lord redirected me.

The long journey to that blessed and merciful transformation was mixed with ups and downs. But my exuberant flings ended in deep depressions, which eventually led me to the dark, cruel corner of skid row. I entered a community hospital through the compassion and influence of the late beloved Dr Bill Holley, and the staff put me in an isolation ward where I was treated for alcoholism. Although comfortable, I felt very lonely and unwanted, and being continually possessed of suicidal tendencies I conceived all kinds of plans for disposing of myself but I just could not complete them. Life was sheer agony, yet, somehow, I had the desire to live.

The only literature in the isolation ward was a Gideon New Testament, which sat on a locker beside the bed. I wasn't too fussy about this. I didn't believe in the New Testament, nor in the stories of Jesus. I was indignant at the presence of the book and mumbled away to myself that more consideration should have been shown to my literary taste. Why not give me a bundle of randy magazines instead of trying to force me into the Bible-thumping brigade. I resolved to protest at the earliest opportunity – although really I had no right even to be in that hospital, with my self-inflicted malady.

But the protest was never made. Sitting up in bed that Sunday morning, something powerful and unseen compelled me to lift the Gideon New Testament. Opening it at random my eyes fell upon Luke 11, verse 9, and this warm invitation: 'And I say unto you; Ask, and it shall be given you; seek, and ye shall find; knock, and the door shall be opened unto you.'

I read the message over and over again and came to the conclusion that it was written for 'down and outs' like me. Almost immediately the wee bits of religion I had learned on my mother's knee and in that back-street mission hall more than fifty years before came back to me vividly, and I could distinctly hear a voice say: 'Why do you doubt Jesus? Why do you doubt His virgin birth? His virtuous life? His miracles? His vicarious death? His victorious resurrection?'

An upsurge of emotion took me, and in my mind's eye I could see Jesus hanging on that Cross, horse-whipped, bleeding from those horrific thorns, and dying in front of that motley crowd of onlookers. Weeping sorely I crawled out of bed and shuffled over to the window. The countryside was beginning to wear its Spring dress. For the first time I saw this as the handiwork of God, and realised He was speaking to me. Closing my eyes I pleaded earnestly for mercy, and suddenly an indescribable glow of warmth and joy overwhelmed me and I knew something wonderful had happened to my wasted life. There and then I had an intuition that I would never drink again!

My reaction to this amazing change was to go round the hospital telling everybody. But after some thought I was prompted to sit down and write a note to Jack, a colleague who was in another hospital with a slight coronary. Jack was addicted to heavy drinking and gambling: he and I had tried repeatedly to steer clear of the curses, but had failed hopelessly. In my note I mentioned my acceptance of the Lord Jesus Christ and concluded thus: 'Jack, I trust that now you will make strenuous efforts to find the same Salvation, for only Almighty God has the answer to soul destroying problems.'

At this juncture I must refer to the Revd. John Beatie, a fellow patient in the community hospital. Each morning and afternoon he sat at a table beside his bed reading a large Bible through an equally large magnifying glass.

Before my conversion I wondered and wondered why an ordained clergyman, aged ninety-two, who should have had the contents of the Bible digested one hundred times over, was still reading it with intense interest. My curiosity knew no bounds! What was there in the tattered old book that this man could not separate himself from?

One afternoon I ventured to question him on the matter and he returned in haste: 'My dear boy, every time I read the Bible I am sure to be the recipient of something new which instils in me solace and hope.' Pausing for a moment he dropped the magnifying glass and went on pointedly: 'And may I also state that this book is a solid rock, and more people, including you, should be concerned about getting a foothold on it so that you may find the pathway to eternal life with the Holy Father.'

Lost for words I moved away from the old man's steady stare. For hours afterwards his reply haunted me. I kept asking myself: 'Could the Bible possibly be a guide to another place beyond the grave?' At that point the controlling evil force within me intimated that I was being soft and silly. But I know now that a small seed of goodness had been planted in my heart that day which, helped by the fertiliser of the Gideon New Testament, eventually produced fruit in abundance.

On the Monday following the Sunday of my conversion I went to the Revd. John's ward, taking with me a banjo that was among my few belongings, and it was then I shared the glad tidings.

The old man's face wrinkled into a benign smile and he murmured: 'It looks like we're going to meet on the Heavenly shore after all, Speedy. Just you keep trying . . . the Lord loves a man who keeps trying.'

Beaming, I held up the banjo and said: 'I know only two Gospel tunes – *The Old Rugged Cross* and *Amazing Grace*. I'm waiting on your request, sir.'

'I think *Amazing Grace* would be nice and appropriate,' came the soft reply.

As I strummed and hummed the lovely air – I didn't know the words – my learned friend's eyes moistened and on the final note he clapped his frail hands.

That was the last hymn of praise the Revd. John Beatie was to hear on earth, for two hours later he was called to his eternal reward.

His final departure from this world was a quiet affair with the cortège consisting of half-a-dozen mourners. But, oh, I would love to have witnessed his reception in Gloryland! I am sure there was a tumultuous welcome, with the greeting: 'Well done John . . . true and faithful servant!'

The first big test to my new way of living came on the afternoon of the old clergyman's interment, and it was really tough.

A publican, whose pub I had frequented for a long time, arrived at the hospital and in a lively, affable manner invited me outside. There he opened the boot of his car. My eyes goggled as they took in bottles of booze galore! I looked at the publican questioningly. 'A wee gift from my customers and staff and me,' he said, 'to prove that we haven't forgotten about you.'

Beads of sweat oozed from my forehead and trickled down my face. Then I heard the voice of evil say: 'Take it and drink it, man – have a good time and get converted all over again.' When the Holy Spirit fell upon me and gave me the strength to say 'No', the publican couldn't quite believe his ears. But he wasn't persistent about me having the cargo of dope. Getting in the car, he drove off shaking his head in confusion!

During the remaining weeks of my stay in hospital the Gideon New Testament became my constant companion, and the pages spoke out with simple clarity to tell me more and more about the great God and His love. I was no longer lonely: a feeling of tranquillity possessed me.

Forever fresh in my memory is the morning I came to John 3:16. 'For God so loved the world, that He gave His only begotten Son that whosoever believeth in Him should not perish, but have everlasting life.'

Those words had a powerful impact on me. I was relieved and thankful to be a member of God's family, for here was His ultimatum to all men and women, leaving them with no excuse on Judgement Day. St John is credited with coining the phrase which has won so many souls for the Kingdom, but it truly bears the signature of Almighty God – the same signature that is written across the sky with its awe-inspiring galaxy of stars, and stamped on the stem of the beautiful, fragrant rose.

Looking back I just cannot understand my stupidity and ignorance, prior to reading John 3:16 and other New Testament passages in that isolation ward. Through the devil's attractions, corruptions and addictions, my eyes were closed to the wonder of the stars, and my mind was numb to what lies behind the amazing birth of a lovely rose in bloom. But now, a complete new creature in Christ, I can clearly see and fully appreciate God's creations, which, in every aspect, are for the benefit of mankind.

I had regular visits from Dr Holley, the Revd. Sam Millar, the Revd. Colin McFarland, William Henry McCracken (a recovered alcoholic), Gideon Kenneth Caldwell, and newspaper man Jim Mercer, and I gained much strength in my Christian infancy through their fellowship. The prayers of those gentlemen were a revelation, and I looked forward with enthusiasm to their visits in my ward, which had so much literature it was fast coming to resemble a Christian book shop.

Browsing over the mass of reading material one morning a topic in a booklet made me think about the first steps of my Christian walk when discharged from hospital. How would I fit into Christian circles? Would I be able to uphold the standards of those people associated with them?

I assumed that all people professing the Christian faith were one hundred per cent sincere. That impression, however, was dampened that very same morning when a loud knock sounded on my ward door.

'Come on in,' I shouted.

Next second, a clergyman unknown to me stood beside my bed. 'Ah,' I whispered to myself, 'more prayers!'

But I was wrong, for putting his hand in his pocket the clergyman, to my surprise, produced a packet of cigarettes and said as he seated himself: 'You don't mind me smoking?'

I didn't answer, for at the time I was trying hard to give up smoking and was pleased at having cut down to five a day. I knew to be a true Christian I would have to beat the habit completely, and I was praying for deliverance.

As the clergyman puffed rings round him he explained that he was on a routine visit to the hospital comforting folk living in the evening of life and that he was thankful for his smoke in the privacy of my ward.

'There's nothing consoles one on this job like a good smoke,' he declared, smiling. He hadn't even offered me a cigarette.

The clergyman then asked what I was being treated for.

'Chronic alcoholism,' I replied, 'But since being admitted to this ward I met that lovely man named Jesus, and He lifted me from sinking sand and not only saved me for Eternal Glory, but healed me mentally and physically . . . praise His Holy Name!'

Momentarily the clergyman was dumbstruck! But when he found his speech he didn't dwell on a spiritual matter which should have been of paramount importance to him as a representative of God and exponent of the scriptures. He changed the subject to sea-fishing, and then, taking the last draw from his cigarette, put the stub in the wash-hand basin and continued with his 'comforting' of the aged patients.

This encounter, out of the blue, indicated to the young Christian in the isolation ward that even men with dog-collars can be keen sharers of the world's so-called pleasures.

On the afternoon of the Tuesday I bade farewell to the wonderful staff of the community hospital. I went along to Jack's hospital, and on entering the ward he occupied was thrilled to observe a radiant smile on his face and an open Bible in his hand. Both clearly informed me that his seeking also was over.

For genial Jack the fog lifted just in time, for early next morning he was found asleep in the Lord. I miss his companionship and breezy patter, but find consolation in the news the Good Book imparts that one day we will have a reunion in the Land beyond the vale of shadows. There we will have no more partings, no more sorrow and no more tears.

Chapter Two

Many people rejoiced at my conversion. Others mocked it. The betting in the pubs was heavy. 'Three to one Speedy will be back on the bottle before Saturday.' 'Four to one he'll be back with us in a fortnight.' 'Seven to one he'll be back with the old banjo before the end of the month. He just couldn't stay away . . . pubs are his life!'

But the gamblers underestimated the saving grace of Almighty God – the same God Who stopped Saul, the Christian persecutor, on his way to Damascus and transformed him into Paul the Apostle. God can do anything but fail, and He had made a good sound job of old Speedy, not only spiritually, but mentally and physically.

My wife Margaret and I had moved into a new wee home away from the old, bitter memories and I was making a genuine effort to square bills I had incurred during my drinking sprees. When business people who had written off my debts years before as 'impossible to recover' were paid in full, they couldn't believe their senses. But they appreciated my new-found honesty.

One evening a neatly-dressed young businessman came to my new home, and handed me a parcel, and left immediately with hardly a word. The parcel contained a beautiful Bible with big clear print – my first real Bible, incorporating the Old and New Testaments. Inside the front cover was written: 'Enquire within about everything. Rodney Lyle.' I gained much from this kind and thoughtful gesture, and later the donor became my firm friend and mentor on the Gospel of the Saints.

But my Christian walk was not all smooth going. No, there were up-hill climbs and twisting corners which I found difficult because I did not put my full trust in God. Let me dwell for a moment on one of my early failures.

Two grandsons, Moore and Derek, were staying on a temporary basis at my new home, and being strict non-believers were keen on embracing the pleasures of the world. Their mother, our eldest daughter Nina, was confined to a wheel-chair through a mysterious illness, and her sons, who were past twenty, solidly maintained that when such a tragedy had befallen a gentle lovable person with eight children there could not be a God.

It was on an unforgettable Friday afternoon that a car stopped at my front door. Then to my horror the two grandsons and the driver of the car commenced carrying cases of booze into my home!

Rushing downstairs I demanded an explanation and was quickly told that there was going to be a disco that evening and would I stop moaning and being a spoil-sport.

I was really angry as the cursed liquid, which had wrecked my old home, was stacked up in the sitting room of my new one. Slowly, I climbed the stairs to my room. The drinking and music went on to the next morning and I could almost hear one gossipy neighbour say: 'Old Speedy is on the razzle again . . . the religion didn't last too long, as I predicted.'

I conceived plan after plan to get rid of my grandsons, but my wife was fondly attached to Moore and Derek, and other discos followed. The same young couples who had attended the first one returned, and certainly let their hair down! There were Ivor and Louise, Drew and Valerie, Danny and Jennifer, and Noel and Betty in addition to my grandsons and thier girlfriends. Because I was so distraught I never once spoke to God about the situation, and the devil kept fanning the flames of my hatred.

Then one morning on the stroke of four I heard a rumbling in the kitchen directly beneath my bedroom. Curious, I got up and slipped downstairs to find Derek sitting reading an old book without a back which I assumed to be a thriller.

I gave him a telling-off for wasting our light, burning our firing and drinking our coffe. He looked up at me pathetically and said: 'Granda, I just can't sleep.' But I was unrelenting. 'If you would stop your running, your drinking and your discos, you'd sleep a lot better!' I shouted, storming back to my bedroom.

Next morning I was still angry as I approached my wife to report Derek's wasting of our light, burning of our firing and drinking our coffee at the ridiculous hour of four in the morning. 'And he was reading an old book without a back . . . some "Cowboy and Indian" rubbish I would imagine,' I added peevishly, grabbing a cup of tea.

My wife quickly crossed over to the kitchen mantelpiece and lifted from it the same old book Derek had been reading. She handed it to me. 'That's the "Cowboy and Indian" rubbish you refer to,' she said sharply.

Turning over the pages of the book I discovered to my surprise that it was a Bible. I was rooted to the spot, a lump the size of an egg rose in my throat as the tears ran down my cheeks in streams.

My wife kept staring at me, but I couldn't reply. Suddenly I felt smaller than a field mouse. I had stumbled badly on my Christian walk through my abruptness and refusal to look towards the Holy Father for guidance. But thankfully the Holy Spirit was striving in our new wee home and my sobriety was witnessing, for two weeks later, Derek committed himself to the Christian faith in the Coleraine Elim Church. And, amazingly, all of the young people who had attended the discos followed him to the foot of the Cross for deliverance from their sins, and today are trophies of grace as they exalt the Name of the Lord!

I am a journalist by profession, and on leaving the old folks' hospital I was asked to resume my human-interest page, 'People and Places', in the *Coleraine Chronicle*. Writing with a steady sober pen gave me confidence and much pleasure.

Wandering around the countryside in search of material I met numerous people of all walks of life, and those who had knowledge of my former drinking habit kindly commended me on my transformation. I didn't hesitate to give Almighty God full glory for that transformation. I emphasised the fact that what He did for me He can do for others, irrespective of the problems they have.

But I must say, and not without concern, that quite a number of those people who commended me felt that Speedy Moore was a special case. As a chronic alcoholic he needed that transformation, whereas they were fortunate in being able to live moderately. Hugh is a good example.

'Yes, Speedy,' he said, 'I have the booze under control. I am strictly a social drinker. I don't beat up the wife and kids and land myself in a lunatic asylum or jail. No, no, I merely go to the wee pub across the street . . . aye, maybe five or six nights a week and have a few gargles, and d'ye know it fairly shortens the winter.'

Pausing to take a drag from his cigarette, Hugh went on: 'And the wife and I go to church the odd Sunday, Speedy, and pay a good few quid to help keep it going. Man, we have a fine wee clergyman. He preached a sermon a fortnight ago that Jesus said: "Let not your heart be troubled, for I go to prepare a mansion for you." Well, ye know, Speedy old boy, that mansion is for my wife Agnes and me as well as the gospel-greedy who think they're the only folk going there.'

Yes, Hugh and Agnes and many people like them are of the opinion that their moderate way of living and occasional visits to church are sufficient to secure admittance to that mansion in the sky. Let me state now that they are interpreting God's Word wrongly. Their fine wee clergyman seens content to let them 'slider' on in life's journey thinking that all is well beyond the grave.

John 3 verses 1, 2, 3 and 16 say clearly what guarantees a place in that mansion of gold. My spiritual passport was put in order the morning I decided to believe in Him Who died for me – the morning I was born again!

As I write I smile on recalling an experience I had with Robin Ward, North West Area Representative of the Northern Ireland Tourist Board. But believe me, there were no smiles when the incident occurred.

Robin had invited me to accompany him to Ballycastle: 'While keeping me in chat you might well get a story or two,' he said, 'for there's lots of interesting characters in the North Antrim resort, where they thrive on the famous dulse and yellowman.'

As it happened I didn't get a story in Ballycastle on that occasion, but gleaned some nerve-wrecking material on the way home, when Robin suggested that we call at the Benvarden Safari Park.

We were warmly greeted by the proprietress, Mrs Louise Stephenson, who led the way into a large luxurious caravan and directed us to be seated in comfortable chairs at each end of a long couch.

Louise and Robin were talking tourist business when a dull thump sounded on the door of the caravan.

'It's just that big nitwit Barry, excuse me please,' Louise said, rising to respond. She left the caravan.

I wondered who Barry was. I soon found out when a huge lion stalked into the caravan and eyed us fiercely.

Robin and I froze stiff as Barry rather impolitely pushed

past my legs, put two giant paws on the couch, and pulled his muscular tapering body on to it, stretching himself into a comfortable position.

I had stopped breathing. I was praying – without moving my lips – that the Lord would protect us as He did Daniel in the lions' den. Barry fixed his gaze on me again, and yawned to show some horrible-looking molars. I just couldn't stop myself shuddering!

At last Louise returned to the scene with coffee. Seating herself on the couch in front of Barry she began caressing his head and nose until he closed his eyes and dozed in obvious contentment.

The lady continued her tourist talk with Robin, but no answers came from him. His sole concentration was on the lion's tail as it went up and down on his knees with the regularity of a grandfather clock pendulum. His eyes were wide in their sockets as they followed the movement. Neither of us touched the coffee.

'Gentlemen, gentlemen,' said Louise, 'you are surely not afraid of Barry? Why, he's as quiet and innocent as a cuddly kitten. Aren't you, darling?' she chuckled, tickling the giant animal's ears.

But in the next minute, to our relief, she hastened to the fridge and bringing a plucked fowl out of it called on Barry to leave the couch. He did so quickly, tumbling the coffee stand and me as if we were matchsticks. Picking myself up off the floor I watched the lion, fowl in mouth, make his exit. I breathed again and offered a word of thanks.

My Christian walk had not, so far, involved me in any evangelical activities. I was attending a midweek Bible study and, of course, church on Sundays, and was quite content to carry on in that lukewarm, sleepy way. All I desired was to remain sober and live a better life. But the Lord had a plan for Speedy Moore.

Seven months after my conversion I had gone to a Reverend Sammy Workman Gospel Campaign in Garvagh, a small town in County Londonderry. My principal mission was to photograph and interview the top Ballymena gospel group, the *Jubiliers*, for a newspaper feature.

The group were participating in the campaign and after I had finished with them and was leaving the hall a gentleman, Tom Thompson, asked me if I would return on the following Tuesday evening and give a word of testimony. I had all kinds of feelings about the request. I couldn't say 'Yes', and I couldn't say 'No'. I just stood there. Eventually the gentleman's persistency won out and I agreed, wondering how I was going to cope with my latest commitment. Standing on a stage was not strange to me, but cracking jokes in a concert was a different matter from giving a testimony.

The next few days were agony. 'What will I say to those people on Tuesday evening?' I kept asking myself over and over again.

I would sit and write and write and write to the small hours of the morning. The result was a basket full of rubbish. In the end the ordeal was getting me down and the evil one was taking advantage of the situation. He even flashed a glass of whiskey across my mind, but I was quick to resist the temptation.

My inability to understand must have hurt God some. I should have known from the scriptures I had read that sincere prayer is the answer to every problem. But I must confess now that prayer was my weakness. Often when I got down on my knees I became tongue-tied. Somehow I was in awe of God. He was so mighty and I was so insignificantly small.

When I looked at the local paper on Thursday morning and saw a brief announcement that I was to testify at the CWU Hall, Garvagh, on Tuesday evening, everybody welcome, another dozen butterflies entered my stomach.

By the day before 'testimony Tuesday' I had actually lost weight. I continued to let the devil have a say, and he was punishing me so much, in fact, that I finally accepted defeat by lifting the phone to tell the Garvagh folk I had not the guts to testify in front of my former pub mates who, I had been informed, were going to attend the campaign for a laugh.

But as I dialled the number the words of Psalm 40:2 suddenly came to me: 'He brought me up out of a horrible pit and set my feet upon a rock and established my goings.' I wept like a child. That powerful force compelled me to drop the phone and I muttered to myself: 'God saved me from the lake of fire, surely He will see me through a simple period of testimony.'

And He graciously did.

It must have been about dawn the next morning that a clergyman rang me at my home. 'I would like your testimony at my weekly after-church rally in the church hall next Sunday,' he said. 'I heard good reports from Garvagh. Will you come?'

The comment lifted my spirits. I promised to go to his meeting and do my best, and this time I did not suffer the tension that I had pending the first testimony engagement. I gave much thought to improving the testimony, and wisely joined in communion with God. I was actually looking forward to the challenge.

The clergyman advertised his rally in the local paper. He featured my name and alcoholic tag more prominently than I wished. But it paid dividends, for the large hall had a capacity crowd and that was a blessing compared to the twenty souls who had attended the previous week.

Smiling and all aglow at the record crowd, the clergyman shook my hand heartily and said: 'For this splendid turn-out we must thank God in the little room at the back . . . come on!'

Prayers over, he studied me up and down and then asked: 'How long is your testimony?'

'Twenty minutes,' I replied.

The clergyman stroked his chin. 'I would like you to cut it to the minimum . . . say five or seven minutes, for I've a lengthy message and a youth fellowship to conduct in Limavady afterwards.'

I was shocked. Being temperamental, I was even thinking about leaving the hall when that force within quelled me and provided a really marvellous liberty.

From that evening I was prompted, through prayer, to don the full armour of God. This was only the first of many knocks I was going to take in the course of my Christian walk.

Chapter Three

It was in Psalm 150 that I saw this passage: 'Praise God with the sound of the trumpet; praise Him with the psaltery and harp. Praise Him with the timbrel and dance; praise Him with stringed instruments and flutes. Praise Him upon the loud cymbals; praise Him upon the high sounding cymbals.'

It touched my heart and set me thinking. I once played a saxophone quite well, first in a number of dance bands and later in pubs where I was assured of a free drink for blowing a tune or two.

Prior to my admittance to the old folks' community hospital I had taken part in a cabaret in a lounge bar. I left my saxophone there overnight. When I went to collect it next day the pub and lounge were a mass of smouldering rubble, the target of a terrorist bomb. I didn't even inquire about the instrument.

As my eyes fell upon the Psalm 150 praise passage again, I was obsessed by a burning desire to play the saxophone for the Lord, so I phoned the proprietress of the bombed pub to see if there was any compensation coming for the lost instrument. To my surprise she replied: 'It's still here in one piece and we were wondering when you were coming for it.'

The saxophone had not escaped intact, but with the aid of a bit of solder and a few rubber bands I managed to play a solo (appropriately, *I Need Thee Every Hour*) at a meeting the following Sunday evening. So in addition to my testimony and messages, I had the banjo and saxophone with which to praise the Lord, and He gave me great liberty on them.

Speaking about that old, delapidated instrument leads me to mention, with fond affection, Mr and Mrs White, who are better known in North West church and business circles as Willie and Mae.

Willie fought in the last war with a famous Irish regiment and he reckoned, like many soldiers, that a booze-up helped to subdue the monotony and, indeed, the sorrow of war. On the cessation of hostilities he was still a young man, but hardened to the sting of death. He had seen many a youngster put in a make-shift grave far from his native land, and he regarded the business of war as foolish and sordid.

The authorities gave Willie a free suit for his return to 'civvy street', but he raffled it in a London pub to buy a round of drinks, so he came home in shirt and trousers.

Willie was really Irish and enjoyed maintaining the traditional reputation of our race. He had no regard for regular hours; no regard for anything except ample laughter, travel and adventure, which he considered proper for the modern man. He remained at home for a few days and then was off again into the blue.

Mae is the youngest member of a large, progressive family. In her parents' home God always had priority and morning and evening His Word was read by a wonderful mother. Therefore, in the process of growing up the lassie inherited strong Christian ideals.

One day, Willie, tired of roving, came home and met Mae. A friendship developed. Nosey observers predicted it wouldn't go far. 'The partnership of an unsettled man of the world and a dedicated Christian girl would never work out,' they said. But the day came when the couple walked the aisle together and their happiness was very evident. Some years later they established a household furniture business. It began in a small shed in the back yard of their home at Portstewart, but with hard work it grew into the largest walk-around store in the county. Willie, under the steadying influence of Mae, turned away from pubs and became a member of a Baptist Church.

He said to me one day in his inimitable manner: 'By your bulging cheeks, that old saxophone seems to need a lot of wind, and an oul' boy like you can't afford to blow too hard in case you burst your lungs . . . Mae and I have ordered you a new instrument and we want you to accept it with our love.'

And so through that lovely Christian gesture I became the owner of a magnificent new saxophone that is easy on the 'oul' boy's' wind, and a treat to play.

On their well-earned retirement, Willie and Mae moved into an imposing old-world mansion. Mrs Frances Cecil Alexander, the famous hymn-writer, lived there from time to time and, it is said, found inspiration for a number of compositions amidst the quietude and surrounding beauty.

'What is the nicest thing that has happened to you during your Christian walk?' That question was once put to me by a dear old silver-haired lady, and I had no difficulty in answering.

The nicest thing that ever happened to me, not only during my Christian walk, but during my lifetime, occurred shortly after my Garvagh testimony.

A few years before my conversion to the Christian faith I had stood at the door of a church hall in my native town, very much down at heel. The Annual Inspection of the 2nd Company of the Boys Brigade was in progress and I had been assigned to write something about it. I'd have preferred to stay in the pub. But as I watched the boys go through their paces I was reminded of the time I marched in the same ranks. At inspections my proud mother was always one of the first parents in the hall. She just had to have a front seat to see her son in action, and in her eyes I could do nothing wrong, even though I did begin the march on the wrong foot eight times out of ten.

From its inception, the Boys Brigade has promoted the teaching of Christian faith, and if a boy takes that teaching in and digests it thoroughly, his anchor will hold in the fiercest of storms. Why had I not achieved the happiness and success of those men I knew who, during their boyhood and youth, had abided strictly by the principles of the Boys Brigade? How did I ever manage to reach my present state of corruption?

On getting the details of the inspection and names of the honoured guests I returned to the pub sad and dejected. Such nostalgic events stirred the emotions of my sick mind and I spent the remainder of the night worrying about my destiny. It was then I recalled an old Brethren man telling me that I was going straight to hell. Was there such a place as hell? Was I not enduring hell upon earth through my mental agony?

Then came the glorious morning I saw the light in the isolation ward and was released from the devil's shackles. The steep climb into decent society was tough and I had my stumbles. The day I really felt I'd made it was the day I slit open an envelope to find a letter from the Captain of the 2nd Company of the Boys Brigade, part of which read: 'We would be honoured if you would act as our Inspecting Officer at the forthcoming inspection.'

'Ma'am,' I said to the old silver-haired lady, who had questioned me as we sat together having tea in the basement hall of Lerwick Baptist Church, Shetland, 'that is the nicest thing that ever happened to me.'

There was no reply. Blimey, she was weeping and so was I.

The Province of Ulster, trouble-torn and blood-soaked, also

has its share of problems created by alcohol, which is advertised through every conceivable medium.

In an endeavour to counteract the awful effects of alcohol – the mental sickness, the heartbreak and wrecking of marriages and homes, and the untold suffering of little children – Dr Bill Holley formed a Christian Group called Alcoholic Victorious. It had been founded in the USA, upon the principles of Alcoholics Anonymous.

On each Thursday evening the doctor opened his private home to alcoholics of all denominations and there we sat, Catholic and Protestant, in true comradeship. All the sectarian propaganda in Ireland would not have separated us, for when one reaches the very bottom of the world in despair one is not interested in a person's religion. All one seeks is a word of comfort.

After converted and unconverted members had shared their everyday experiences the doctor would read and expound some passages from the Bible. And at an interval, Mrs Marian Holley, the doctor's charming wife, would serve a homely cup of tea and delectable home-baked fare. The good doctor encouraged us to pray aloud individually in turn. I remember asking God to reunite Johnnie and his wife Susie (I am using fictitious names); Ellen and her husband Sam; Willie and his wife Myrtle; Alex and his wife Molly. Many of our members had suffered broken marriages. Big Jimmy and his wife Nan had a marriage more broken than most.

When Big Jimmy arose to pray he rhymed off: 'Lord, by all means reunite Johnnie and Susie, Ellen and Sam, Willie and Myrtle, and Alex and Molly, but as far as my wife Nan is concerned, please, dear Lord, keep her away from me as far as you possibly can!'

What could we do but laugh, and I am sure the good Lord joined us. The person I refer to as Big Jimmy had an appalling prison record, all through drink. But one day he joyously accepted Christ. Really, another Divine miracle had been performed.

The majority of our members had tried everything under the sun to escape the curses and agonies of alcohol. They had been to lunatic asylums, nerve hospitals, monasteries and prisons, but they only found the peace of mind which passeth all understanding when the Lord Jesus Christ came to them and said 'Wilt thou be made whole?'

Dr Holley had the thrill and great joy of pointing Arthur Williams to the Lord. Arthur, an addicted two-fisted drinker, had gone to the doctor's private residence, pleading for something to cure the effects of excessive drinking. The kindly doctor gave his patient a prescription, and, as he was walking towards the door, smiled and said: 'I can give you a much better and more permanent cure than the one on that piece of paper.'

Arthur stopped. 'What other cure have you, doctor?'

'The Lord Jesus Christ.'

A chat ensued and eventually Arthur rolled the prescription into a tight bundle and threw it in the fire. Then, kneeling beside the doctor, he became a completely new creature in Christ. He went on to study at a Bible College in England, and later was inducted as Pastor of the Finlay Memorial Church, the second largest church in Glasgow. Apart from his pastoral duties, Arthur did splendid work among Scottish alcoholics which resulted in him forming the Stauros Foundation, now world-wide and taking a strong stand against the evils of drink – the devil's easiest method of destroying souls.

Dr Holley and a dozen members of his Irish group attended a Saturday Night Rally for alcoholics in Arthur's church in 1979, and we never will forget that visit until the breath leaves our bodies.

We travelled by Larne and Stranraer. On the ship we distributed Gospel chorus books to our fellow passengers and I led a session of singing on my banjo. Even the lips of the card-sharpers were seen to move to the lively lilt of *When the roll is called up yonder I'll be there*, although group member Paddy annouced that they hadn't a chance of being there unless they reformed.

A man with a Canadian accent, who had clearly had a few, produced a small drum and sticks. Certainly his drinking did not impede him from sending out a true beat and lending yet another sweet voice to the choir. Between choruses I explained to him that the tough-looking guys in our party, singing their heads off, were recovered alcoholics, saved by the Grace of God. He reckoned I was shooting a line of Blarney.

The Canadian traveller followed us on to the Glasgow-bound train and continued to give me a beat on the drum. I noticed that he was sobering quickly and, at last, I got a chance to speak to him about Jesus, and what He had mercifully done for me and my comrades. He believed me this time. Indeed, he showed an eagerness to have our permanent sobriety and peace. I prayed with him and Jesus dispelled the trouble in his soul.

I laid my head back for a little doze, visualising the rejoicing of the angels as they entered a new name in the Lamb's Book of Life. When I awoke my Canadian brother in Christ handed me a piece of a brown paper bag and a poem scribled on it. It will hardly take a place beside the works of the master poets, but the sincerity and feeling with which it was penned qualifies it for a place in my heart and in this narrative. It may be sung to the tune of *The Rose of Tralee*.

I walked the false paths and I heard the wrong drummer,
My heart was despairing, my soul was not free,
I came to the Lord and He's guiding my footsteps
Away from the thoughtlessness and selfishness in me.

Oh He's loving and fair and He made me a promise
That someday in Paradise with Him I shall be,
Enveloping love among all of His chosen
Is mine just because He died for me.

Henry Rainey,
Bracebridge,
Ontario.

We walked miles and miles around Glasgow, seeing the sights, and people everywhere were most hospitable and jolly. This attitude was so different from the fingers of scorn that were once pointed at us in our drinking spells. What a change the Lord has wrought in our lives! It was great to feel wanted.

At the end of the day our feet ached as we returned to the homes of our various Christian hosts. Said one member, who had slept rough in rat-infested derelict buildings, cow sheds and barns for seven years: 'I was kissed on both cheeks going into the house and I was up to the ankles in carpet in the bedroom, which I had all to myself. I was attended hand and foot and kissed on both cheeks coming out of the house. In the end I had to pinch myself twice to see if this was really me and not the prodigal son.' And he was speaking for all of us.

The Saturday Night Rally in Brother Arthur's church was a huge success with a capacity crowd. Dr Holley was a very capable chairman and in the course of the evening he called on two or three of us to testify. The closing message from Pastor Williams was a challenging one. The result was an astounding twenty-six souls finding salvation!

We were all deeply perplexed and saddened when later the news of Dr Holley's illness reached us, and the afternoon I met Mrs Holley shopping in Coleraine was a particularly trying experience for me. 'Bill is sitting in the car outside your office,' she said, 'go down and have a chat with him.'

I hastened to Marian's car and found the doctor sitting in the front passenger seat. Smiling, as usual, he motioned to me to join him.

Slipping into the driving seat I faced my friend, not knowing what to say. But the silence didn't last too long, for without beating about the bush and with tremendous courage and with no signs of the radiant smile fading, the doctor said: 'I'm for heaven, Speedy. I have contracted an incurable ailment, Motor Neurone Disease.' Shrugging his shoulders, he added: 'It's just a matter of time.'

My eyes filled with tears and the doctor, who was always an expert at comforting, put a hand on my shoulder. 'Don't let this matter disturb you, Speedy,' he said softly. 'This world is not our home and we have all got to leave it at some stage . . . the important thing is being prepared for the next one.'

The doctor seemed to have resigned himself to the strange ways of Providence and he quickly changed the subject to our new Recovered Alcoholics' Christian Fellowship. Even sickness had not dampened his enthusiasm for the group's successful future. All the powers of my dear friend's unique personality were spent for the social and moral betterment of the downtrodden – alcoholics who were the victims of their own folly.

Bill Holley made a full commitment to the Christian faith in Newtownards in 1942. He served in the second world war as a Surgeon Lieutenant in the Royal Navy, and resumed his civilian medical duties after demobilisation in 1945. It was in 1947 that Dr and Mrs Holley went to serve as missionaries with the Qua Iboe Fellowship, at Ochadamu Medical Centre and Leprosy Settlement, in Nigeria, and remained there for thirteen years, facing many challenges. Apart from the satisfaction of assisting in the treatment of dreadful diseases, the young couple rejoiced in many people finding a new life in Christ.

Returning to Northern Ireland in 1961, Dr Holley became a General Practitioner, and latterly was the medical officer at Magilligan Prison, where he involved himself in Prison Fellowship and marvelled at God's power in redeeming souls and uniting them across religious and political divisions.

At a special service in Portstewart Baptist Church, prior to the doctor's interment, I saw hard men, alcoholics and converted terrorists of different persuasions, shed rivers of tears. We are immeasurably the poorer without him.

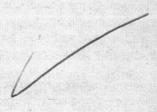

Chapter Four

During my Christian walk I was quick to notice that many people in my home town of Coleraine, and neighbouring towns, never entered a church door. 'How can they be brought under the sound of the gospel?' I kept asking myself. 'Surely there must be a way of interesting them in the Word and the lovely songs of Zion?'

Putting the matter to the Lord I was afterwards impelled to book the Coleraine Town Hall, for a Saturday night 'Spiritual Feast', with the main view of enticing those non-church-goers and pub-crawlers to attend.

There was no trouble forming an orchestra, for I was in touch with a number of converted dance band instrument-alists, including the brilliant partnership of Tom Hyde, on piano, and James McKeown, organ. Soloists, duets, trios, quartettes and choirs came easy, for singers seem to grow on trees in Northern Ireland.

The big problem was getting a first-class speaker for the epilogue. Then Willie and Mae White came to the rescue by obtaining the services of the dynamic Pastor Willie Mullan. His name alone assured me of a capacity crowd. God was with me in the venture, for everything was going according to plan – ample musicians, singers, stewards and general helpers, and now a great preacher!

Coleraine Town Hall stands imposingly in the centre of a large diamond, and as I prepared the spacious interior for the 'Spiritual Feast' I was conscious of the prominent part the same hall had played in the great Ulster Christian

Revival of 1859, which was sparked off by four young men in the village of Connor, County Antrim. They began praying fervently and were later joined by others, for morality in the Province then was at the lowest possible ebb and evangelical religion in the churches dull and sparse.

The Revival spread like wildfire and there were cases of both men and women in Coleraine 'stricken' unconscious because of their sense of sin. The Spirit of God was in their midst as never before. Let me quote a *Chronicle* file of June, 1859.

> 'We have again to crave the indulgence of our kind friends for the absence of many matters intended for this day's paper. We are in the midst of the most marvellous and exciting events ever to take place in Coleraine. We have witnessed scenes, and taken part in some of them that have entirely incapacitated us from collecting our thoughts on any other subjects.
>
> 'God is in our midst and we have seen the manifestations of His power. No pen can adequately describe what has been transpiring in this town and neighbourhood since our last issue. It would require to be seen to be comprehended.'

In that particular era the Coleraine Town Hall had just been completed, so someone suggested it as a fitting place of shelter for the many people who wouldn't go to bed during the Revival spell. This was immediately acted on and permission was granted and the hall remained open day and night for prayer and hundreds of people came to Christ under its roof. As I spaced the chairs in the ancient building for our meeting I looked back on its initial use in the service of the Lord and prayed and prayed for yet another Religious Revival – the only cure for our sick land.

On the Saturday evening of the 'Spiritual Feast' crowds

thronged the Coleraine Diamond, and the popular preacher had a job on his hands trying to squeeze into the hall. But oh my, how Willie Mullan addressed that really super audience. During his message one could honestly have heard a pin drop. He was great, and people didn't want to leave the hall.

Other 'Spiritual Feasts' were promoted in Portstewart, Portrush, Limavady, Ballymoney, Ballymena, and Maghera, and this is where I must recount a little bit of history of my Christian walk, which I am not likely to ever forget.

I had also been taking part in meetings throughout the Province and Eire, and at each I experienced a real feeling of peace and warmth. Saying farewell to folk at the end of fellowships was like bidding adieu to family members. Among numerous Christian friends of mine is Mrs Georgina Linton, of South Londonderry. When parting, the lady, like so many others, held her cheek for me to press a kiss upon it.

At one of my 'Spiritual Feasts' in Portstewart Town Hall I was welcoming people when in the distance I saw Georgina, wearing that lovely smile that endears her to everyone. So delighted was I to see her that I rushed down the steps with arms outstretched and lips pursed for the usual kiss. But Georgina was strangely stiff. No sooner had I reached her than the smile disappeared from her face, and releasing herself forcibly from my embrace, she took two steps backwards. Indeed, I was of the opinion she was going to call a policeman!

It was then I discovered that Georgina has an indentical twin sister, Miss Philomena Brown.

Was my face red? But when an explanation was offered the lovely smile returned to Philomena's face and we became staunch friends. And there can never be another mistake, for I kiss both twins now.

Pastor Willie Mullan came to speak at our special meetings often and our only problem was finding seating to accommodate the huge crowds that attended them. He loved staying with Willie and Mae White at Dundooan House. The old Georgian mansion was so interesting and relaxing, and many a sermon was put together within its precincts.

The two Willies and Mae were strolling along the beautiful Portstewart Strand at midnight, getting some fresh air after a meeting, when Mae was prompted to ask the preacher: 'What experience would you cherish most on life's journey, Willie?' Almost instantaneously the reply came: 'To come face to face with my Saviour.'

We will always remember with affection that Lurgan pastor.

The Revd. Sammy Workman, widely known and much loved for himself and for his extraordinary ministry, was another 'hall-packer' we were honoured and delighted to have as a speaker in Portstewart.

Sammy and I have been good brothers since I first met him at his Garvagh Campaign in late 1976, and as I did a press profile on him I learned that he wasn't always evangelically inclined. Oh, no, if someone had predicted to the Ballymena lad, in his teenage years, that he would wear a dog-collar and preach the Word one day, it would have given him a fit!

Sammy, an exceptionally good ballroom dancer, would have travelled miles for a 'hop', and possessing a striking personality and a keen sense of humour, his company was much sought after. One evening in early 1950, Sammy and a good pal were, as they thought, boozing merrily, in a Ballymena pub. But as the pal left to go home to his wife and family, he dropped dead going in the door.

That tragedy completely changed the outlook of Sammy Workman. To the surprise of his friends, he dedicated himself to God and gave up everything in the world to train and then serve with the Faith Mission. Later, he studied for the ministry and eventually went as minister to Abbot's Cross Congregational Church, Belfast. Each Sunday evening people of all denominations came from different parts of the country to hear the Gospel preached in a unique and spirited manner. Finally the minister from Ballymena was led to devote his full-time to evangelism.

Since that calling Sammy Workman has carried God's Word to many places in the world and through the mercy and love of Almighty God, he has brought peace to thousands of disturbed souls.

I was very pleased to have Hedley G Murphy as a friend and mentor. Good fortune decreed that I was to meet the great evangelist in Portstewart. He had gone to the town hall for something and I had gone to the town hall for something else, and we collided with each other. But we mutually agreed that the collision was arranged by the God we both loved, for almost immediately I began assisting HG in the Lord's Work.

The Lord had called Hedley into world-wide evangelism. It happened the day my friend went into a Bible shop, and there, printed on a card were these words: 'The Lord hath chosen thee. Be strong and of good courage and do it; fear not nor be dismayed, for the Lord God, even my God, will be with thee. He will not fail thee, nor forsake thee until thou has finished all the work.' (Chron. 28:10-20).

Hedley was a gifted speaker and, of course, a principal figure on the *Irish Gospel Radio Hour* from Monte Carlo. In 1962 he visited the Radio Station there and had one week in conference with Christian leaders from thirteen different countries. He found it an education listening to their personal stories of trial and triumph in the field of Radio Evangelism.

Hedley was a most interesting conversationalist and he could tell a good joke which had us in fits of laughter. Time in his company simply raced. His preaching and Bible prophecies packed halls and large marquees in all parts of the country, and it was a great experience for me to be associated with his annual summer Portstewart Crusades, in the spacious town hall.

Every single minute of those meetings was a source of spiritual profit for the thousands of people who attended them, and as I testified and played solos on the saxophone, the liberty was tremendous. The Holy Spirit was certainly present.

One Friday evening proved to be very special for me. I was sitting on the platform prior to the commencement of a HG Crusade, and the evangelist was telling the mass audience about a trip he was conducting to the Holy Land the following week. He strolled in a leisurely fashion down to the body of the hall, whilst our ensemble played a selection of rousing choruses.

But Hedley came back to the platform hurriedly. 'How would you like twelve days in the Holy Land, leaving next Saturday, and free?' he asked me.

'Pull the other leg, mate,' I said, running my fingers through my hair.

But the preacher was on the level. A fellow I had served with in the forces in the last war, and who had made a success of his life spiritually and financially, was so pleased to see me in God's service that he paid Hedley £600 there and then for a ticket. So I joined the party of eighty for a dream holiday.

The flight from Heathrow to Tel Aviv was smooth and uneventful, but on touching down on the Holy Soil an upsurge of excitement gripped us all, for in this small country lie the ruins of the world's most ancient civilisations. From its environs spread the rule of moral and religious beliefs, enlightening people blinded by error and idolatry.

In ancient times pilgrims came from every land, enduring fatigue and discomfort and braving all kinds of perils, just to worship here. Today pilgrims still come in vast numbers to stay in the finest of hotels, ride in luxury coaches and swim in three seas – the Dead Sea, the Sea of Galilee, and the Mediterranean.

I can say now how glad I am to have had the opportunity of going to the Holy Land with Hedley Murphy. Readers will sense the joy that filled us as we walked around Bethlehem, the birthplace of Jesus; Nazareth, where He grew up; Capernaum, centre of His ministry in Galilee; the Mount of Beatitudes, on which He preached His famous sermon; Tabgha, where he fed the five thousand; Cana, where He turned the water into wine; Jericho, where He called Zacchaeus down from the sycamore tree; and the Mount of Olives, the place of His ascension into heaven. The describing of these Biblical scenes was an extension of our leader's evangelistic ministry, and tourists actually accepted Christ as they followed in His footsteps.

At the barren rocks of the Gadarenes I was reminded of the lunatic in Mark 5, who had to be bound in chains. But as those chains were forged on his arms and legs he snapped them with supernatural strength, and in the end the authorities decided to isolate him. And believe me, they really did isolate him when they sent him to that place. I wept for the man, having known a wee bit about isolation myself.

Mark goes on to tell us how Jesus arrived on that remote shore of the Gadarenes and brought peace to the lunatic's sick and tortured mind, just as He brought peace to mine in that isolation ward, two thousand years later. It was just a matter of history repeating itself and proving that Jesus is very much alive!

The trip was bearing fruit for me. There were times when I was treated to a wee bit of unconscious humour from the natives of Israel. In a café on the shores of Galilee, I saw a basinful of fish which looked like our Irish mullet, only much smaller. I learned that they are nicknamed 'Peter's fish' and when I tried to explain to the proprietor in my slowest English that in our rivers back home there are tens of thousands of similar fish, the length of your arm, with no one interested in catching or eating them, he replied in distinct Cockney: 'Paddy, boy, you haven't only kissed the Blarney stone . . . you've taken a big bite out of it!'

Hedley Murphy was a strong supporter of the Israeli cause, and solidly maintained that it was God's will. In a lecture on the Plain of Armageddon he said: 'Israel is the only spot on a cursed earth that God calls "My land", and people ask: "Should Israel give back to the Arabs the land she took from them?" A careful reader of the Bible will understand that Israel cannot part with that portion of land, not even when threatened with an armed force of two hundred million.'

'Why, why?' we asked.

Hedley smiled and went on: 'Israel today is exactly what God intends her to be – 1,600 furlongs in length. That is very significant, for in Revelation 14:20, it simply states that in the last days of the Battle of Armageddon, Israel will be 1,600 furlongs in length, so when the Israeli Army pushed back the boundaries of the land from Mount Hermon to Eliat in the 1967 war, it was really God's miracle.'

We were enraptured with our leader's commentary as he continued: 'While most of Israel has been built on with housing, offices, universities, etc, the Mount of Olives has been left in its natural state. No one has been able to build there, to mar or destroy it, for the Bible says: "His feet shall stand on that day upon the Mount of Olives".' The speaker wagged a reproving finger at us and concluded: 'And remember, on that great arrival the land is to be 1,600 furlongs in length . . . are you all fully prepared for the second coming?'

In 1983 I could clearly see Hedley Murphy's health deteriorating. A diabetic, the man was doing a mountain of work. His medical advisers were always trying to put the brakes on him, but to no avail. When he lost his sight I could never quite describe the feeling of sadness that possessed me. I kept asking myself: 'How did this ever happen to a man of God?'

Indeed, I ventured to put this to Hedley one day and he simply replied: 'A trial of faith', and then referred me to Job in the Bible.

This man of courage was also attacked by strokes which took toll of his limbs, yet he remained non-complaining. We were all deeply impressed with his Christian example. At one particular Crusade in Portstewart he was helped into the Town Hall by two brothers in Christ and sat in the back row. He couldn't see, he couldn't talk, and he couldn't walk, so his presence affected the large audience emotionally.

On the platform were a High Court Judge, a barrister and a headmaster, but I didn't hear one word of their testimonies. No, my thoughts were fully with my dear brother, his sightless eyes welled with tears. I was glad to see the end of the meeting, and sleep didn't come easy to me that night. However, by the will of God the great evangelist recovered sufficiently to walk, unaided, on to the platform of the Portstewart Town Hall at a special Rally the following Easter, and speak to a vast crowd of admirers. He was superb.

A short time afterwards, Hedley Murphy, greatly used of the Lord in the salvation of souls and in the ministry of God's Word, went to be with the Master. It will be good to see him again in that new body he so often told us about.

* * *

Joe Black, born and re-born by grace in dear old Donegal, is known the length and breadth of Ireland as the 'Wandering Preacher'. The 'tag' suits him, as he certainly does roam far from his wife Jean, his son Andrew, and his comfortable Ballymena home.

Jean, a schoolteacher by profession, is the noted gospel singer, whose record and tape ministry brings brightness and joy to thousands of folk in all parts of Britain and Eire, and when her itinerant husband conducts a meeting within reasonable range of Ballymena, she assists him.

The story is told about Jean and her schoolboy son, Andrew, sitting around the fire on a cold winter's night, the head of the house missing, as usual. Full of curiosity Andrew said: 'Mummy, I wonder where the fire goes to when it goes out?' To which Jean replied: 'You might as well ask me where your daddy goes to when he goes out!'

Joe Black's ministry knows no boundaries. Before his more organised and precise system of holding meetings he would drive his old Ford car into an isolated mountain district, eye and count the houses and cabins, then approach a farmer for the use of the barn, potato shed, or hen house, which he never failed to get, thanks to his persuasive line of chat.

The preacher would then throw the coat off and, if necesary, scrub the building from top to bottom with disinfectant, install his portable pulpit and organ, borrow seats, and go round the countryside telling men, women and children about the Gospel Rally in 'Paddy Murphy's' barn, commencing on Sunday evening and continuing until further notice.

Joe once conducted a mission on top of a mountain and a fussy singer was really annoyed at having the task of driving his car up the almost perpendicular, muddy track. Arriving at his destination, a big shed, the singer commented sourly: 'That's a long, nasty, muddy oul' track, Joe.'

'Aye,' returned the preacher, 'but sure, if it was any shorter it wouldn't reach.'

I didn't quite know how to assess my future with the 'Wandering Preacher' after the very first meeting when I had testified for him in the Ballymena Faith Mission Hall. It was the final night of a three-week mission he had conducted very successfully, and he had prepared a farewell message. And it is not often Joe sits down and studies and makes notes for a sermon, so good and natural is his impromptu style. But this was a special occasion and he had a lot to say to those people who had crowded into the large assembly room.

As I rose to testify the preacher whispered: 'Finish in ten or fifteen minutes, for I don't want to keep these people here to the morning . . . I follow you with my message.'

Well, I just cannot explain what happened to me that evening in Ballymena. I could not find an ending to my testimony and went on and on and on and certainly there were no signs of restlessness from the folk in front of me. The unrest came from those behind in the pulpit who almost had the jacket pulled off my back. I believe I managed to finish eventually with a strum on the banjo.

The 'Wandering Preacher' got up, large Bible in hand, and said: 'With his own allotted span, Speedy has also taken mine and I trust the miracle of his testimony has sunk deep into your hearts.' Glancing around the big gathering he made an appeal for souls for the Kingdom and then called the last hymn.

At supper time I had a guilty feeling about my long-windedness and promised Joe that there would never be a repetition: which, really, was inviting myself to another of his meetings, in which liberty reigns supreme.

In eleven years I have participated in many Joe Black campaigns throughout the Province of Ulster and Eire, and the esteemed 'Wandering Preacher' never again put me on a time schedule. He introduces me thus: 'I'm going to turn Speedy loose now and the rest of the evening is his if he wants it.' And every campaign I have attended, whether in barn, potato shed, hen house, hall, tent or church, has been packed to the seams.

Indeed, the very last meeting of Joe's at which I testified to God's saving grace and power, was in a spacious barn away in the wilds of Donegal, and lovable folk from old-world villages, mountains and green valleys flocked to it and had the thrill of seeing an alcoholic, who had lost everything, come to Christ Jesus.

Joe Black is a delightful companion. He is wonderfully humorous and never permits dullness nor monotony to affect a congregation while he has a funny snippet up his sleeve. And, oh my, what a lovely way he has of expressing them.

With a serious face he once recalled a morning he went into a Donegal School to give a half-hour of religious instruction to the pupils.

For his subject he chose Noah, and called on a boy to say how he figured Noah and his passengers passed away the hours, days, weeks and months afloat in the ark.

'I would imagine, sir,' answered the boy, 'that with so much water around them they would do a bit of fishing.'

Just then another bright boy jumped to his feet and shouted: 'Sir, they wouldn't do too much fishing with two worms!'

I love the innocence of the story of the two Donegal Sunday School teachers – a boy and a girl who had eyes for each other, but were very shy.

At length the boy picked up courage and asked the girl if he could take her home after a fellowship meeting and she agreed, and so the friendship went on for eight months.

One beautiful night, when the full harvest moon shone

down on the young couple as they strolled towards the girl's home, the boy said: 'Patricia, can I hold your hand?'

'No thanks,' replied Patricia, 'It's not heavy, I can hold it myself.'

But foremost in the 'Wandering Preacher's' ministry is the Gospel of the Lord Jesus Christ, and he has spent most of his life proclaiming it and sowing fruitful seeds along the way. I trust God will continue to use the energetic Joe, and Jean, and Andrew for many years to come.

When I go across-Channel or abroad I am always sure to be asked by curious people if I have ever seen Dr Paisley in the flesh and I am not too long in informing them that I have not only seen him in the flesh, but that I know him well personally.

On hearing this, one startled Yorkshireman spluttered: 'By gum, would he be similar to what Dr "Gobbles" once was in the propaganda and trouble-brewing spheres?'

Yes, there are misguided people who picture Ian Paisley as a kind of Dr 'Gobbles', a firebrand gospeller and a political fanatic, who wishes everything to go his way. Admittedly, he is loud and bitter in his public debates, but his critics do not seem to realise that he is fighting for a cause he believes in.

The English press has never been kind to Ian Paisley, and some of the pieces I read about him have turned my stomach. Yet the imaginative journalists have written without having interviewed or spoken to their subject, which, I feel, justifies me in expressing my opinion of him. And I am not one of his flock, nor am I over-keen on politics.

As a very old newspaper hog, I've had an eye on Ian Paisley since his ordination to the ministry in 1946 and the birth of the Free Presbyterian Church of which he is moderator. I have not always agreed with his policies. But, in fairness, I have found him to be a man with tremendous foresight and his predictions, over the years, have been amazingly accurate.

A dedicated Ulster-Scot, he is strong in body and mind, is self-reliant and persistent and, in response to the blood that flows in his veins, adventurous. From boyhood, under the care of sterling Christian parents, he had a passion for education and religion and was strict in morality. And Ian Paisley is not without a sense of humour. He can tell a joke and listen to one with equal enthusiasm. I have often stood on platforms before audiences using his name in jest for my entire performance, and the loudest laughter of all came from his Reverence and his wife Eileen, sitting in the front row.

Dr Paisley and I met frequently when he was contesting the North Antrim parliamentary seat which he won with a staggering majority, and I remember getting the successful candidate into a corner where I popped the question: 'How are you, a gentleman of the cloth, going to make politics and church activities mix harmoniously?'

The reply was: 'I sense danger and there is no way I'm going to stand by with my hands tied and see Ulster being sold. It is only through the medium of prayer and strong action that I can help. When all is well I will gladly leave politics.'

And let me say that the big man is a true friend and servant to all of his constituents, Protestant and Catholic. I have spoken to Roman Catholics who would have no other representative. He gets things done for them immediately, and they are grateful. That's a nice wee tit-bit the English press failed to print about the firebrand gospeller.

Ian Paisley knew all about my heavy drinking and said, with deep concern, that if I continued it would lead to tragedy. He was right. When he was told of my conversion in the old folks' hospital by Alderman James McClure, he was the first cleric to send a message – 'We were praying for you and we're still praying. Congratulations. Keep moving forward with the Lord.'

The thrill of a lifetime came when Dr Paisley invited me to testify in his Martyrs Memorial Church, Belfast, at a special Good Friday meeting. And as I stood in the pulpit taking in those three thousand faces which seemed to get smaller and smaller until they disappeared into the roof space, I felt the size of a tiny mite.

But the Doctor's formal introduction already had me well-received by the international congregation, so speaking was much easier. And, of course, the Lord was on my side. Without His support and guidance I would have been hopelessly lost in the immensity of such an occasion.

How Ian Paisley keeps going baffles us all. He is in the Northern Ireland Assembly at Stormont; he is a Westminster MP, a European MP, and an outstanding Preacher of the Gospel who never fails to deliver two sermons in his magnificent church each Sunday.

His name, associated with any function, is sure to draw a massive crowd. Just recently I had him all to myself in a room at Magherafelt Technical College, prior to us taking part in a Praise Service, and I was quick to recount the day his Reverence entered a lone farmstead in a mountainous area of North Antrim, soliciting for a vote. Sitting in front of the turf fire was a pet pig named Topsy and she was enjoying the heat. Rachel, the old woman who worked the farm, was so pleased to have such a personage as the Doctor in her kitchen that she lifted the black teapot from the heathstone and poured tea into a bowl and handed it to him.

As the vote-hunter reluctantly sipped the strong tea, the pet pig began to scream its head off. The Doctor turned to the old woman is distress.

With a smile and a shrug of her shoulders she replied:

'Pay no attention to Topsy, your Reverence, she doesn't like anyone else using her wee blue bowl.'

We laughed heartily together, for both of us like a bit of fun away from the hustle and bustle and the sometimes exhausting strain of everyday life. Then the Doctor commenced telling one to beat mine, but before he finished we were called into the big hall. Hopefully, the duel will be continued at a later date.

Chapter Five

The Salvation Army is one movement I admire, for when we servicemen were in the thick of war, an SA mobile canteen was always convenient for a bowl of warm, stimulating soup. And on weekend furloughs in the towns and cities of England and Scotland, poorly-paid soliers were assured of the comfort of an SA hostel – and a bed and cooked breakfast for one shilling. I often made use of this service, and greatly appreciated it. Therefore, when I was invited to speak in the Salvation Army Citadel in the Borough of Ballymoney, County Antrim, I was pleased to accept and went along with a stock of pleasant wartime memories.

At the finish of the lively meeting I was approached by an athletic-looking chap whose bright smile spread from ear to ear.

'Remember me?' he asked.

'Well, well!' I exclaimed, 'Bobbie Dunlop, who played in the dance band with me.' I stroked my chin and studied the other calculatingly. Forty years is a mighty long time, yet Bobbie Dunlop still looked the same old 'ninepence' in spite of a whitish-grey mop that had taken the place of the auburn threads I knew.

The last time we had met was at a dance in Castlerock, away back in 1939. But after that the athletic-looking chap with the auburn hair suddenly disappeared from the dance band scene. I often wondered where he had gone. Then the second world war separated me from the homeland for five years, followed by an unprofitable spell in Australia, where I had taken full advantage of wine at three shillings a bottle and turned out to be a tramp.

Bobbie and I arranged to meet in his home, which stands on the ancient family farm on the outskirts of Ballymoney. It proved to be a nostalgic occasion. It was like old times as we played our instruments together again – only our choice of music this time was spiritual and not of the world, thank God.

That memorable evening I listened intently to the story of my long-lost friend's conversion, and I was captivated. At last the missing years were linked.

In 1939, Bobbie Dunlop, aged nineteen, was of the opinion that he was born to take a prominent place under the spotlights of the entertainment world. He performed all over the country, arriving home regularly at the dawning of the day. The rural dances and harvest balls contined until five o'clock in the morning, and at one Bobbie, who was the MC, quite literally called the last dance at 5.30 am. A big farm labourer, sweating in profusion, shouted: 'Hi, Bobbie, we don't start our work until seven o'clock. Keep the fun going!'

One summer's evening, Bobbie Dunlop observed, without the slightest interest, a mission tent in a field near to his home, and a couple of Faith Mission pilgrims making preparations for a four weeks' stay.

Out of curiosity the budding dance band musician strolled into a tent meeting. He paid little attention to the service, and wasn't sorry when it was over. He figured that visit and the silver sixpence he put in the box coming out would be his sole contribution to the event. he just couldn't afford another evening away from practising the latest dance band music. That was more important than a dull mission.

But much prayer was going up for the saving of my

friend's soul, from family members who were concerned about his impetuous way of living. And God heard the earnest pleas and answered, for Bobbie visited the tent again. That evening he was puzzled why he had come to yet another meeting, for the preacher's last message had failed to stir any emotion within him. Then came the closing hymn, and as the touching words and beautiful melody rang throughout the canvas interior, Bobbie Dunlop, the wayward youth, was suddenly under conviction.

> I've wandered far away from God;
> Now I'm coming home;
> The paths of sin too long, I've trod,
> Lord I'm coming home.

During the singing of the last verse and chorus his eyes were tear-stained.

> My soul is sick, my heart is sore —
> Now I'm coming home;
> My strength renew, my hope restore —
> Lord I'm coming home.

> Coming home, coming home,
> Never more to roam;
> Open wide Thine arms of love —
> Lord I'm coming home.

Bobbie Dunlop knew perfectly well that if anything had happened to him at that particular time he wouldn't be going home to be with the Lord, his great Creator. So he got washed clean in the blood of the Lamb and wrestled himself from the fears of tomorrow. The born-again youth commenced working for the Lord almost immediately. For a period he was associated with the Belfast City Mission, witnessing around the docks and back streets, and helping down-and-outs and telling them in his own appealing manner about Jesus and His love.

The occasion of our reunion in the home of my long-lost friend was to prove quite significant, for it was then we formed a partnership that was to travel to many parts of the province and Eire, and see precious souls saved.

Bobbie is a second-cousin of the Formula One World Motor-Cycle Champion, Joey Dunlop, and when he was driving to meetings I was convinced that he thought he was Joey, for there's only one thing would have passed us on the road – a telephone message! Speaking truthfully, I felt safer when my friend's affable wife, Gretta, was at the wheel and doing the map-reading, for we never got lost in her charge. And Gretta, also a gifted pianist, organist and singer, greatly enhanced our ministry with her gracious presence.

Bobbie and I had many exciting experiences which space does not permit me to relate, but I feel there is one worthy of mention – one that further glorifies the saving grace and power of Almighty God.

We had been asked to take part in a Gospel Concert, and my partner, being a strict Presbyterian Church Elder and a Sunday School Superintendent, wasn't one hundred per cent keen on those mid-week ticket promotions, whilst I, still a baby in the faith, willingly appeared on all kinds of platforms and stages, delighted at having the opportunity of demonstrating God's goodness to me before vast inter-denominational audiences.

After some consideration Bobbie came to the concert. And apart from reciting poems of his own composition, singing in a sweet natural tenor voice and playing violin solos, he was also an excellent chairman. Ignoring the printed programme he called upon me to close the concert with a word of testimony and I have never enjoyed better liberty as I finished with *How Great Thou Art* on saxophone, a tune beautifully suited to the instrument.

When the hall emptied my attention was drawn to a couple of young men standing in the middle of the hall and a woman further down at the door. I moved towards the men, and could see by their bleary bloodshot eyes and suffused countenances that they were victims of alcohol.

'We are in desperate trouble with the booze,' one said, 'and my mate here is just out of a mental asylum . . . how do we go about finding the sobriety and peace you have?'

I invited the men to be seated and began: 'Fellows, there's no sense in me wasting your time and my own time by shooting a lot of hot air about this matter of life and death. The only answer to your horrific problem is the Lord Jesus Christ, and He is waiting to help you right now.'

The other young man who had been discharged from the mental asylum, and who was six stone in weight, explained that the woman at the door was his wife, that their home was being broken-up the following Monday through a legal separation, and that the authorities were putting their four children into care. He went on to tell me about the debt the booze had put him in, and that he couldn't see how conversion to the Christian Faith would solve his difficulties.

'My son,' I said, putting an affectionate hand on his shoulder, 'you have got to pull yourself together, trust in God, and strive to keep your wife and kids.'

I described my own debt headaches, which were a lot bigger than his, and assured him that if he genuinely entered God's family circle he would be gloriously redeemed and given strength to face the future.

As the alcoholics and the woman left the hall I said appealingly: 'Please do not lay your heads upon a pillow tonight until you make matters right with God. He will see you through this turbulent spell and give you peace.'

Bobbie and I prayed for the trio and found the fruits of our efforts in abundance a couple of months later. We were speaking and playing music at a men's Monday night Bible Class in Belfast, and almost jumped with joy as we saw our two alcoholic friends sitting in the front seat, and looking spic and span with open Bibles in their hands. Another young man, without a Bible, sat between them.

At supper-time, Bobbie and I listened to three experiences that only the Holy Spirit could have created.

Going home the night of the Gospel Concert, the first man and his wife had stood in front of an empty fireplace, staring at each other. Without speaking the wife slipped into a bedroom and the husband went to another. When they met again in fifteen minutes they had both accepted the Lord Jesus Christ into their hearts. As man and wife embraced with new-found love and tears of joy streamed down their cheeks, they determined in the Name of Christ to save their home and their children. With God's help they did, and the people of the neighbourhood marvelled at the transformation and helped them in every way.

The other alcoholic had a similar victory over evil. But my story is not yet ended. The fellow who sat between the two converts was a brother of one, out of prison on parole. He had come to the Bible Class seeking the peace and happiness his brother had found. Bobbie counselled him, and when the prisoner returned to his dark cell the following Tuesday, he was a complete new creature in Christ.

During our long car journeys throughout the country, Bobbie Dunlop continually referred to two dear friends – long since gone. He loved to keep their memories fresh, and I loved hearing about them. They were the Revd. WP Nicholson, and one of his converts, Johnnie Herbison. I know it will please Bobbie to say a brief word about them.

WP, as Mr Nicholson was affectionately known,

exercised a world-wide ministry as an evangelist and writer, and the gospel he preached was that of repentance and faith. No allowance was made for a middle course or compromise, and the result was a crop of vigorous converts. An Ulsterman born and bred, WP pointed thousands of sinners to the Lord in all parts of the world, but he reckoned that Johnnie Herbison's conversion was the most remarkable of all.

Johnnie was born in Ballymena in the latter part of the last century, and I am telling his story principally in the hope that those alcoholics are still in one piece will take warning and repent. Johnnie's mother died when he was a small child, and as his father drank like a fish the boy grew up wild and undisciplined. Since his uncles were horse-dealers, he too began working with the animals. About 1910 horses were kept in the yards of most Ballymena pubs, and this gave fifteen-year-old Johnnie access to as much strong drink as he wanted. Soon it took control of him and his rebellious ways were beyond curbing.

One night Johnnie got mixed up in a street brawl. He was too intoxicated to remember what had happened, but the terrible result was the loss of an eye, which had literally been kicked out of his head. Then sometime afterwards, tragedy struck again in the worst possible way. In a drunken state on a rainy afternoon he struggled into his dimly-lit room and bent over to take off a shoe, never realising how close he was to the pointed brass knob of the ancient bedpost. As his head went down the knob smashed into his good eye and completely shattered it!

Johnnie was in a predicament, for in those days a blind man was not allowed Government aid of any kind until he had reached forty. Alas, no one would employ him. But the one degrading place he did not want to be put in was the Workhouse. So at length he devised his own method of making a living. He somehow managed to get a donkey and cart and began selling fish around the streets. It was amazing how he found his way; but he did, and he developed a prosperous little business by working hard and keeping sober.

Soon he had saved enough money to purchase a pony and trap and in a short time he included fruit and vegetables in his enterprise. But after this spell of sobriety and progress the street trader began to drink again, and in a matter of weeks had lost everything and was so swamped in debt that he was forced to sell the pony and trap. He was in a desperate situation, and all through drink.

Mercifully, at this time WP had come to conduct a mission in Ballymena. After attending a few of his meetings the blind sinner got saved and, daily, he commissioned the neighbours' children to read Bible passages until such time as he learned braille. In 1928 Johnnie Herbison married, and from the union there were six children. His wife, Nellie, gave him every help and encouragement.

He had commenced making things with his hands in an effort to make a living. But his real opportunity came when a carpenter who lived next door kindly offered to show him how items of furniture were made. When his knowledge and skill increased, with the aid of one or two special devices such as a notched rule for measuring and a sawing guide, he set up a workshop of his own and began to take orders for a wide range of household furniture. Later, and miraculously, he made pony carts and caravans. For nearly half a century this gifted and happy man played his accordion and mandoline and testified in every corner of Northern Ireland. A favourite phrase of his was: 'The devil and his solution took my eyes, and the Lord gave me my hands.'

Bobbie Dunlop and I are exceptionally friendly with a young Ulster preacher who answers to the name of Edward

Totten. I say 'young' because although the man is a centenarian, he is non-stop action, and would take two meetings in an evening if asked.

Once upon a time, while passing through Edward's native Ballynahinch, we decided to call at his home and get a close-up of what really makes him tick. We were received warmly by our friend's daughter, Mary, and later learned that daddy was soon to celebrate his one hundred and third birthday. Then the preacher himself made his appearance and seeing us he turned to Mary and said: 'Make two sups of tea for our guests . . . 'tis not too often we see them.' He then sank into the comfortable depths of his favourite chair and engaged us in conversation, changing the subject from time to time in pleasing and understanding continuity. Our hosts's striking personality shone through, and we felt very much at home in his company. When he referred to me as a 'mere boy', I was completely rejuventated. In fact I'm over seventy!

Edward Totten opened his eyes to the blue skies of Glassdrummond, on 6th August, 1883, and began toiling on the land at an early age. In that far-off era attending school was not as important as it is today. Neither was it compulsory. The Government's policy was to see children of farming stock producing food. Young Edward soon became a skilled ploughman. Few men in the country could handle a pair of horses like him. He took part in ploughing matches in different parts of the north and won many cups and trophies.

It was in 1931 that he totally committed himself to the Christian faith, and he gives thanks to Almighty God for his longevity, good health and full faculties. People have come to an Edward Totten meeting for the sole purpose of seeing a man of one hundred and three. In other words, for the novelty. But they have gone home richly blessed and with a greater knowledge of the Good Book.

The centenarian's memory was incredibly sharp, and he was untiring in his efforts in praising God to the highest. I doubt whether there was another preacher in Europe, or indeed the world who, at such a ripe old age, could have expounded the gospel so impeccably.

One morning in April, 1987, while perusing the contents of a local newspaper I was saddened to read of the death of my friend in his 104th year.

In recalling our happy fellowship meetings and the old man's brave stand for everything pertaining to the glory of God, I could clearly visualise his triumphant entry into Heaven, and amidst the rejoicing, someone shouting: 'Move over there Gabriel, here comes Eddie Totten . . . at last!'

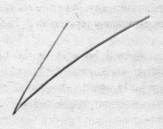

Chapter Six

Evangeline Booth of the Salvation Army once said: 'Drink has drained more blood, hung more crepe, sold more homes, armed more villains, slain more children, snapped more wedding rings, twisted more limbs, dethroned more reasons, wrecked more manhood, dishonoured more womanhood, broken more hearts and driven more to suicide than any other evil that ever swept the world.'

How true! Today, Britain and Eire are certainly having their share of the aforementioned scourges. Seldom is there a day that passes without me hearing of a man or woman in dire trouble through drink. I could fill the remainder of my book with shocking stories of suffering and downfall.

Yet the road to despair (and finally hell) for those wretched victims of alcohol began, perhaps, when as pure unsuspecting boys and girls they accepted a seemingly innocent glass of sherry or sparkling champagne at a Christmas party.

Pastor Charles Hosteller, in his radio *Mennonite Hour*, put the dangers of alcoholic beverages in their true perspective when he told the story of two boys who were met by a dog as they approached a house.

One said to the other: 'Go ahead and open the gate. The dog is OK – look, he's wagging his tail.'

To this the second boy replied: 'Yes, he's wagging his tail, but look at his teeth and listen to his growls.'

They didn't know which to believe, the friendly wagging tail or the warning growls. Drink always appears very friendly and tries hard to make us feel that one is out of date, a poor sport, a social misfit, a kill-joy, if one refuses.

Tragically, multitudes believe the friendly wagging tail and ignore the warning growls until they are caught and enslaved. How factual is this philosophy of Pastor Hosteller. He went on to say: 'Strong drink is a corrupter of public morals and outrivals all other causes as a trouble-maker. It also heads the list as a spoiler of character and waster of fortunes. It is the devil in solution.'

I was greatly perturbed with the Northern Ireland drink situation. In comparison with any other part of the UK, we had a much larger percentage of alcoholics, many of them teenagers.

How could I ever forget the Saturday morning I heard a loud moaning coming from a stinking, derelict building as I strolled along a back street of my native town. I entered to see a man lying in a cold, damp corner. His bed was two sheets of cardboard, with another piece of cardboard on a flat stone for a pillow.

He was hopelessly intoxicated and going through an unconscious, slovenly motion of rubbing swollen purple wounds, with pus oozing out of them, on the shin of his right leg. I later learned that a nearby grocery gave this social outcast the ends of cheese slabs to sustain him, as any Government relief he received was spent on cheap wine.

When he got down on his cardboard bed eating the cheese, sometimes he sank into a drunken sleep. It was then the rats appeared. They feasted in style, leaving nothing of the cheese-end but the piece between their host's fingers, They were most precise in performing this operation.

But one afternoon a couple of daring and curious rodents crawled up the sleeping drunk's trouser leg. Immediately he was brought to his senses. He grabbed the bulky form of the intruder at the top of his thigh, and held on grimly while the second rat escaped, leaving a set of poisonous teeth marks on his shin.

Still holding the squealing, wriggling rat, which he hoped to smother with his trousers, the drunk managed to get up and make his way to the Samaritans in the next street. He too was squealing with pain and fright. By the time the duty Samaritans opened the door the rat was lying dead on the pavement, but, like the other fiend, it had left terrible teeth and claw wounds.

It was the horrible rat wounds he was rubbing the morning I found him. He was still in pain even though the Samaritans had taken him to the Casualty Department.

I studied the dishevelled wretch, and lapsed into reverie. I had known him as a fine schoolboy, full of promise, and later as a smart soldier, who had served throughout the Second Word War. But the bottle of cheap wine at his side had lowered him stage by stage to a degrading existence of prison cells, mental asylums and cardboard beds in derelict buildings. He had an appalling record of ninety-two drunken offences.

But one day the social outcast sobered, and that evening he came to a meeting in the home of Dr Bill Holley. Dr Holley extended a warm welcome, and made him feel like a human being. To our delight he cleaned himself up and remained sober, and eventually, in answer to our prayers, was allotted a small flat. There, one unforgettable day, counselled by a Christian lady social worker, he kneeled and fully accepted Christ.

Today, my friend is doing splendid work in the temperance sphere in schools and youth centres, and as he pulls up his trouser leg to show the ugly scars, the result of the rats' visitation, he demonstrates the bitter depths of despair drink can lower a person to, and then in the next breath praises God for His mercy and goodness in delivering him from the gutter.

* * *

Through the Lord's grace a prison ministry was opened to me, and I found this most rewarding, both at home and across the Channel. I always had my old banjo with me, and on one occasion in a tough prison I asked a large audience if someone would select a chorus for the road. A big 'lifer' put his hand up and shouted: 'Give us that old favourite, *What a Friend We Have In Jesus*. And thanks for coming. If I don't see you one day on the other side of these walls I'll see you in the land beyond this cruel world, for the Lord has saved me for Eternity . . . hallelujah!'

The Holy Spirit is moving in our prisons and more and more men and women are coming to know Christ. One of the most impressive and encouraging meetings I have been to was in a Scottish Young Offenders' Centre and I am certain a number of members of the juvenile congregation were saved that evening, for the liberty was really indescribable.

Outsiders – Christians among them – shower scorn on prison conversions. I have heard some people say that a converted prisoner has a better chance of remission, and he or she will thus profess Christ for the wrong motive.

I do not agree with this view. It is a form of judging, which in God's eyes is sinful. Take, for instance, my very good friend Charles 'Chuck' Colson, one of the officials closest to former President Nixon. Chuck was jailed for his part in the Watergate crisis, but found peace and strength in Christ, which caused widespread bewilderment. Could this hatchet-man and tough ex-marine possibly have become a 'Bible-thumper'?

Yes, many people throughout the world suspected Chuck's transformation was a gimmick. But it was only too real. During his stretch inside, God led him to dedicate his future life to a full-scale prison ministry, which resulted in the forming of Prison Fellowship – an organisation doing marvellous work in the spiritual interest of those misguided souls behind bars in almost every country of the world, and to helping those who are newly discharged in their life outside.

Chuck Colson held an International Conference at Queen's University, Belfast, in which I had the pleasure and honour of taking part. Bishops and high court judges from as far away as New Guinea were present to commend the service of the Fellowship.

When Chuck returned to the States, he sent me a letter of thanks and a signed copy of his excellent book *Born Again*. I treasure both. I can say without the slightest doubt that God is using this man mightily as He is many other prison reforms.

My first television appearance as a Christian was in the programme *Sunday Insight*. I had twenty-five minutes all to myself to tell how God saved me from disaster. But whilst I knew by the many letters I received from people of all denominations, and all walks of life, that the venture had proved fruitful, several people said I should have had more respect for the Sabbath Day.

But at all times God is my guide, not man, and without Him I couldn't pass a pub, so I know it was with His love and blessing that I sat before the cameras on that memorable occasion.

My next television spot was with Sir Harry Secombe in *Highway*; again I had the opportunity of testifying to God's saving grace and power, and again I was inundated with letters from all parts of Britain and had the joy of pointing a viewer with an alcoholic problem to the Lord.

After that nation-wide programme came my crowning glory – an invitation from Gideons International to speak at their annual Conference in Birmingham, in the coming April.

However, another television part on the national network almost turned out to be quite ignominious for me. Let me explain. I do a lot of salmon and trout fly-fishing on the ample waters we have in North West Ireland, and with some success if conditions are suitable.

One day my phone at home rang and a cultured English voice said: 'I'm producing a television film about River Bann activities and would like to include a fly fisherman casting. You have been recommended for the job . . . will you be good enough to co-operate?'

To cut a long story short, I agreed to bring my boat along to just beneath the famous Bann salmon fishery and keep casting in the background while the camera crews captured shots of the tall majestic trees, the flora and fauna and the colourful bird life and, of course, the jumping salmon. It was an easy and pleasant assignment, though I knew I had no chance of catching a fish on that particular stretch of water.

I watched the scenery. As short distance away stands the old Loughan Parish Church of Ireland. Associated with it is John Watt, an extraordinary man, who must hold a world record because he is church organist, choirmaster, sexton, bell-ringer, and gravedigger.

Twenty minutes passed, and then the television producer and director interrupted my casting and called me ashore. I soon discovered what was afoot. There in a bin the couple of crafty sods had a live salmon from the fishery. They quickly hooked it on to my line, and set me and a cameraman adrift on the water.

I did not like this unsporting and cheating act, and neither, I am sure, did the mass of spectators lining the embankment. But there was nothing I could do but play the gallant fish, which I eventually netted and dropped into the boat. With a red faced I posed beside it while the camera raced through to the end of the bogus scene.

On being dismissed from the ordeal I moved slowly down the beautiful river which has given me countless thrills over the years, my poor old sporting heart dull and sad. If that sham film in which I had just performed appeared on the screen, the local community would know I had not caught that fish, and so in my embarrassment I prayed and prayed to God that the lie should escape me, for the sake of my Christian walk, which was straight and steady.

As it turned out, the next day a cameraman on duty on the upper regions of the river got an excellent shot of an angler sporting a salmon which had put up a terrific fight. As I viewed the film I breathed a sigh of relief. I remained in the background, casting gracefully amidst the grandeur of nature. I could with a clear conscience continue to recite my favourite stanza.

> God grant that I may live
> To fish until my dying day,
> And when it comes to my last cast
> I then most humbly pray,
> When in the Lord's safe landing net
> I'm peacefully asleep
> That in His mercy I be judged
> And good enough to keep.

I first met the Revd. William McCrea through taking an alcoholic to a mission he was leading in Maghera, and such was the inspiring message he conveyed on the occasion that the shaking booze victim was first in the queue at the counselling room door before the appeal had finished.

A strong temperance man, as all clergymen should be, William McCrea maintains that Ulster's troubles are not just in the conflict of Republicans and Loyalists – the slavery of alcohol has a lot to do with them. He is also much concerned about the British Medical Association's tests proving that any youth who drinks four pints of beer a night for eight nights – or two thirds of a bottle of wine, or three 'doubles' of spirits – will have caused damage to his liver.

This frightening news has the reverend gentleman praying constantly for the many young people he knows, between eighteen and twenty-five, who drink far more than this and over longer periods. They are at risk from the dreadful disease, cirrhosis of the liver, which is curable only through the grace and mercy of God.

William, a Stormont Assembly member and a Westminster MP, has joined those of us who are endeavouring to take the fight against alcohol into our Primary Schools. If we do not get the vital truth to the children, we are going to see an appalling number of alcoholics in the coming generation – the result of breweries and distilleries advertising their devil's liquid freely through every medium under the sun.

The conversion of my alcoholic friend at William's mission that evening was quite sensational. But as the clergyman and I discussed the victory outside the hall afterwards we little realised that God had a plan for the pair of us to combine our musical talents and use them in His service at Praise Rallies throughout Northern Ireland.

William was born on his father's farm at Ballywholan, County Londonderry, in August 1948. Actually, I could be his grandfather, but if you saw us working together, you would say we were brothers, simply because his lively company has made me young at heart. I'm not boasting when I say that William McCrea and I always get good applause from audiences, whether in the huge King's Hall, Belfast, or a barn in the wilds of the country.

When an opportunity to tell a joke offers itself to this popular man of the cloth he often tells it at my expense, for he reckons that folk need a good laugh now and again. And I am quick to retaliate by telling a funny story about him. A favourite is about the time he was under church, municipal and parliamentary pressure, and went to his specialist for a tonic.

'William, boy,' the specialist said, 'You've got to relax and take things easier. Get your rod and do some fishing ... there is nothing better for releasing pressure on the mind.'

'Where will I fish nowadays with so many water restrictions?' the clergyman asked.

'On my private stretch at Carnroe on the River Bann,' the kind specialist answered. 'You can be my guest for as long as you wish.'

Carnroe offers the best salmon fishing in Europe. Shortly afterwards, when I met William at a petrol filling station, he said with excitement: 'I caught a salmon this morning and it was forty-two pounds. In fact when I got it on the bank the river lowered a foot!'

I, too, was wearing angling gear and after I had commended William on his good fortune, he asked me: 'Did you catch anything?'

'Oh yes,' I replied, 'I was fishing at the Giant's Causeway, near to where part of the Spanish Armada foundered four hundred years ago. I was bringing in my lure when the point of my rod bowed in courtesy to something big. After a struggle I got my catch up on the rocks to find that I had hooked one of the lanterns of the old battleship *Gerona*. The candle was still burning!'

'Absolutely preposterous!' William exclaimed, 'That is a confounded lie.'

'OK, William,' I returned immediately, 'I'll tell you what I'll do ... you take thirty-six pounds off your fish and I'll blow out my candle!'

The Revd. McCrea is a Free Presbyterian Minister in charge of the beautiful Calvary Church, Magherafelt. Rumour has it that Free Presbyterians are clannish and

and always in a recruiting frame of mind. Well I am not a Free Presbyterian, yet I have always been warmly welcomed in their circles, and no one ever asked me to become a member of his church. But one thing they do advocate is that everybody should be saved for the Kingdom.

William McCrea and his wife Anne are a devoted couple, and have five bonnie children, who are following in mum and dad's Christian footsteps. In their home I can clearly see and appreciate the essentially happy dispostion and enjoyment of life, in spite of William's busy activities and travelling.

The Revd. William McCrea, of course, is known throughout the English-speaking world as a leading Gospel singer, and his many albums, most of them made in Nashville, USA, are simply an extension of his ministry. He continually receives letters from people everywhere who have been gloriously born again through listening to his records and tapes in their homes.

I am delighted and privileged to have the McCrea family high in my list of friends, and I will always be grateful for their fellowship and support during my Christian walk.

Chapter Seven

From the beginning of my Christian walk I had often been asked if I had any written material on my testimony, and this prompted me to produce a booklet *To God Be The Glory*, to which the late Pastor Willie Mullan kindly contributed with an excellent foreword.

My personal comment was: 'If just one solitary wretch reads this narrative, by chance, and is delivered from the curse and horrors of alcohol as I knew them, then every hour I spent writing it would be justified.'

Today, thank God, I could touch on quite a number of conversions to the Christian Faith – in prisons and out of prisons – as a result of the booklet. Let me relate one briefly.

Jim lived in the east of the Province. An alcoholic of the worst possible type, he was a source of torment not only to himself but to his young wife and six children.

One morning he went on a drinking spree, taking the car without regard for the dangers intoxication creates on the roads. Strongly under the influence he entered a busy thoroughfare and, not surprisingly, hit another vehicle.

The culprit didn't stop and so the police were alerted and joined in a nerve-wracking chase. In the end the hit-and-run driver was cornered, but he would not surrender, so a fisti-cuff battle ensued in which a police sergeant was assaulted. The points were mounting against the accused. He was in dire trouble this time, and nobody would suffer more for his stupid folly than his wife and kids.

Jim was locked in a police cell to cool off and sober.

When leaving the station next morning a Christian inspector gave him a copy of my booklet. The policeman had no great expectations. But the alcoholic, with shaking hands and full of shame and remorse, read about the miracle of my conversion, and a glimmer of hope entered his heart.

On the following Monday morning he returned to the police station, expressed his deep regret at what had happened, and apologised. Then he asked to see the Christian inspector, who had given him the booklet.

The duty constable told the visitor that the inspector was prosecuting at the Court House, so he walked across to the judicial building in which he himself would shortly be on trial and waited until four o'clock in the afternoon, the time the inspector finished.

Jim was in tears as he pointed to the booklet and said: 'I want to find the same peace as the writer of this . . . maybe you can help me?'

The inspector quoted appropriate scriptural pieces, and then prayed, and Jim, the alcoholic, reformed in the lovely name of Christ Jesus within the precincts of a Court House. Now he could face the trials and tribulations of the future with renewed strength.

Later, Jim and his wife and family became pillars of Newcastle Baptist Church, County Down. Presently my friend is studying at Bible College. This is truly the work of the Lord.

Pretty Emma Jane Good and I fell deeply in love at first sight the evening we were introduced. The main reason was that we were both authors. It is most gratifying being an author – even in a small way.

Emma, the daughter of Revd. Peter Good, esteemed pastor of Lurgan Methodist Church, and the equally esteemed Mrs Jane Good, was just nine when her book

Dear God was published. It sold 13,000 copies with the proceeds going to the Northern Ireland Council For Orthopaedic Development, a local voluntary organisation which cares for physically handicapped children and adults. The Council pioneers development by providing diagnosis, treatment, training, residential accomodation and general welfare, so it is really a first-class cause to support.

Emma came into the world in a hurry! Born prematurely eleven weeks before she was expected she weighed only 2lb 2oz. When a year old she was diagnosed spastic. But thankfully it was soon observed in the growing-up years that the child was gifted with intelligence and understanding and that she possessed immense charm and other sterling qualities which made her a firm favourite with school friends. Speaking for myself the child's natural winsome manner wove a spell over me like a soothing tonic and induced in me a feeling of gratitude for the benefit of sound limbs.

Emma, small of stature but big in spirit, courageously shows us that difficulties are made to be defeated. The well-known Ulster author and journalist, Alf McCreary, describes her thus:

'Everyone has his or her own story and in that sense each person makes an impression. Yet there are a few whose courage, or insight or personality can leave an idelible mark.

'Such a person is Emma Good, who has brought much joy to a life where others might have seen only difficult circumstances.

'In her book Emma demonstrates the simplicity and yet the profound wisdom of a child-like faith. She cuts through the barriers of denomination, theology and the stuffiness of so much church life to present a witness to a living Gospel!

'Emma's words have the freshness of the special person who is far beyond her years in perception and who possesses the rare gift of seeing our old world through fresh eyes. To read her words is to understand perhaps, for the first time, what Christ was trying to convey when He talked about the Kingdom of God, and the devastating simplicity and faith of a little child.'

A documentary film was produced on the day to day doings of Emma Good, and it has been shown in many parts of the world as an example of the Irish colleen's tremendous faith and serene happiness, which can only come from the God she loves.

The child's book *Dear God* comprises the prayers she offered from her very tender years. Here are a few.

Dear God,
Thank You for Mr Piggot, my specialist. Be with him when he operates on my ham strings. May I not be too lonely in hospital. Bless mummy and daddy and Jennie and Andrew when I am away. Amen.

Dear God,
I know that I am a spastic and that I can't walk, but I know that it is no one's fault. Some day I will walk on my own. Thank You for helping me each day and for giving me lots of strength. Amen.

Dear God,
It is Autumn and the leaves on the trees in our garden are turning brown. They look lovely. Bless all the blind children who cannot see them. Help them always to feel happy. Amen.

Dear God,
You must be sad when You see people fighting. Many

people are lonely because their friends have been killed. We are sometimes home late from school because of bomb scares. Forgive us all and help us to love each other. Amen.

I really enjoyed reading Emma's book of prayers, and I learned a lot from each one. The sincerity is very evident; and I sensed the pen moving under Divine guidance. It was beautiful and most inspiring.

In an earlier chapter I told my readers about the nicest thing that happened to me during my Christian walk. Now I would like to refer to the nicest gesture – the one I hold precious in my long lane of memories.

The Revd. Brian Liddell, now retired, was the minister of our family place of worship, First Coleraine Presbyterian Church. He was a real Samaritan to me before and after my conversion.

First Coleraine is a very old church with a history going back to 1613. In my agnostic days I attended it only on the occasions of family marriages and baptisms.

The week following the publication of my booklet was the Presbyterians' Temperance Sunday, so Mr Liddell invited me to speak for thirty minutes in his church. I could not refuse such a dear friend, although I was nervous, knowing only too well that the Lord Jesus Christ Himself testified in John 4:44 that 'a prophet hath no honour in his own country.'

The clear view from the high pulpit made me more nervous, especially when my roving eyes took in the familiar faces of a solicitor and a bank manager who had hunted me continually for money I had owed in the bad old days. But again God Almighty was with me every second, and when the service ended there was a general congratulatory response. Even the solicitor and bank manager gripped my hand, shook it heartily, and wished me well.

Yet that morning's worship in First Coleraine Church was one of mournful remembrance for choir member, Dr Winifred Fitzsimons, it being the anniversary of the death of her husband, the Revd. Jim Fitzsimons. Flowers had been placed beneath the pulpit as a token of the widow's lasting love.

On arriving home from the church for lunch, I was seating myself at the table when a gentle knock sounded on the door. I answered and standing there was Dr Fitzsimons, her arms filled with the beautiful memorial flowers.

'Your testimony this morning deeply moved me,' the brilliant GP said, then smiling she handed me the flowers adding: 'I want you to have these, which would also have been my late husband's wish.'

I must let it be known now that Dr Fitzsimons' gesture came at exactly the right time in my Christian walk, for seemingly the surprise, or should I say the novelty, of the old drunk's conversion had worn off some folk who, previously, had shown much interest in my future. I was floating in a kind of 'no man's land' – a precarious state indeed. I had prayed for a diversion from this situation, and God provided one through the good graces of his servant, Winifred Fitzsimons. Her thoughtful and kind act completely lifted me, and set my feet more firmly on that rock.

Dr Fitzsimons joined her husband in heaven in August, 1981, after a trying illness. The text from 2 Timothy 4:7 – 'I have fought a good fight, I have finished my course, I have kept the faith' – used at the farewell service could not have been more appropriate. I will never forget her.

I've already mentioned Mae and Willie White, who created a furniture empire and spared my wind by buying me a new saxophone. Their young son, Barry White, was in the sales department of the business and doing well. In getting around he was often tempted and yielded to the attractions of the world, particularly the drinking side.

But the time came when the furniture rep changed, and marching up to mum and dad, said: 'I hope you don't mind. I'm leaving the business . . . I've got a leaning towards the church and I am going to study for it.'

Mae and Willie didn't argue, but supported and encouraged their son in every way, so he went to do an extensive theological course at Bible Temple college, Portland, Oregon, USA.

Today, the Revd. Barry White, his wife Margaret, and three children, Sarah, Judah and Joel, are back home in Northern Ireland and are gloriously happy. Barry, thanks to mum and dad, has taken over Dundooan House, and holds prayer meetings and services there several times a week with a fellowship of more than a hundred brothers and sisters.

The old mansion has a spacious function room in which the famous hymn-writer, Mrs CF Alexander, and her bishop husband and friends often had get-togethers. It provides a nice atmosphere for worship, especially when the two big log fires are thowing out their red glow in the grip of winter.

People from different parts of the Province are still talking in joyful terms of the Crusade Barry organised in the Coleraine Town Hall last springtime. The building was full each evening to hear the gifted ex-furniture sales director, and his great friend and former tutor, Dick Iverson – senior pastor of Bible Temple church, and one of America's best known evangelical preachers.

I was pleased and honoured to be associated with the Revd. White's Christian Crusade in a press role. The people I notified seemed to have got the message, going by the attendances. It was really a joyous experience seeing folk, old and young, coming to know the Lord.

As a youth beginning his preaching career thirty years ago, Dick Iverson possessed a burning desire to travel. And so, closing his eyes, he put a pin into a world map to decide the venue for his initial preaching tour. The pin landed on Northern Ireland, and in a short time the young American arrived there wondering what lay in store for him.

He has happy recollections of the welcome accorded him then, and on his return to participate in the Barry White Crusade, he looked forward to renewing old acquaintances.

Now the story can be told that when Dick had hitch-hiked his way back to the US after that first ever evangelical tour three memorable decades ago, he resumed helping his father, Pastor LN Iverson, in a little church with less than twenty of a congregation. But in 1961 LN Iverson suffered a massive heart attack, and his son Dick and wife Edie found themselves functioning more and more in a pastoral role. The church has become known as Bible Temple, and presently, with Dick as senior pastor, it is vastly enlarged with a magnificent dome and a growing family of three thousand. In addition to its worship the splendid church has a Bible College, elementary and high school, world-wide tape ministry, thriving Christian education department, book-store, publications department, prayer ministry, music department, missionary families on the foreign field, outreach churches, ministries to prisons and to juvenile detention centres, two rehabilitation homes, and much more.

From the immensity of the Bible Temple complex comes a lovely wee tale of romance involving a pretty Irish colleen and an American boy.

Elizabeth Watt was born in County Tyrone, and grew up with the urge to travel and see other places in the world.

One fine day the pretty colleen carried the fascinating soft brogue of mid-Ulster into the cosmopolitan community of Portland, and was received with a very special warmth.

Being a devout Christian, her first thought was to find a church, and after several visits she chose Bible Temple.

Fellowship was plentiful and inspiring, and Elizabeth's faith strengthened. Then something nice happened to her. She met the church administrator, Jack Louman, a young man who had achieved considerable academic success at various colleges, having gained BA and Dip Ed degrees.

The Irish collen and the American boy got in each other's way as much as they possibly could, and in the end they married with the best wishes of the Bible Temple congregation ringing in their ears, and the union being acclaimed generally as 'just perfect'.

During the happy courtship, honeymoon and inseparable partnership, Jack learned much about Ireland and its beauty from Elizabeth, and he knew the time was coming when she would pop the question, 'Why don't we spend a holiday in the old country across the Atlantic?'

Jack, of course, had mixed feelings concerning the matter, for American television and press continually emphasised the troubled image of the Ulster Province, giving viewers and readers the impression that it was an unsafe place to visit.

But Elizabeth had an answer for all that unfair publicity. She kept talking until her persistency won, and not only did Jack come, but also his mum, Mrs Wanda Louman of Washington.

They were the guests of Barry and Margaret White. Jack, thrilled with our golf courses, spent most of his time knocking the wee ball around them with Barry, while the female trio invaded the shopping centres and relaxed on the golden beaches.

I had fellowship with Mr and Mrs Louman, and Mrs Louman senior, and their company was really enjoyable.

They left Northern Ireland with a lot of happy memories to share with their relatives and friends in the States.

Gripping the hands of Elizabeth and Jack, I wished them continued happiness, and expressed hope that more than a fence would run round their garden – bless them.

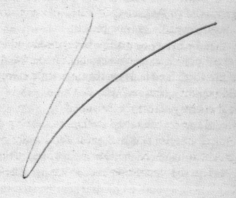

Chapter Eight

Victor Hutchinson requires no introduction from me. He is known in numerous homes the length and breadth of Ireland, and in other countries, through his records and cassettes. Indeed, in 1985 he was awarded a silver disc in recognition of 25,000 sales.

A singer and an accordionist with a hearty and rousing style, Victor played in a dance band until he came to realise that if he was to enjoy eternal life on the right hand of Almighty God, he would have to better his ways of living. He did, and quickly transformed into one of Ireland's leading witnesses for the Lord, not only in music, but as a gifted speaker.

Victor, a Government social worker, was doing a course in London in connection with his job, and while he was there he joined South Norwood Baptist Church. One evening during a youth fellowship hour he met Rosemary, a student nurse, who later agreed to change her name to Mrs Hutchinson and settle in Ireland, where she is a part-time midwife, and seeing to it that her own three fine children, Janet, Catherine and Christopher are growing up with the Lord as their guiding light.

When I was saved from my life of sin and corruption by God's grace, Victor Hutchinson showed his delight and suggested that we combine our instruments for a big meeting he was invited to in Stranraer, Scotland. Without hesitation I said I would go, for I love Scotland and its 'aine' folk. After all, we Ulsterites are very much akin. Take, for instance, North Antrim and the Aghadowey district of County Londonderry, where the natives speak with a distinct Scottish accent and are inordinately proud of the fact.

The Stranraer meeting was a huge success and opened the way for a four-day Gospel tour of Galloway. In the line of beauty, nature has certainly done a lot for that place. Comprising the Counties of Wigtown and Kirkcudbright and the southern part of Ayrshire, the very name Galloway has a lilt to it, and within its boundaries there exists a variety of countryside that suits, so to speak, every mood. Landward, there are scenes as emerald green as Ireland's north west and, seaward, there are fine sandy beaches, seemingly everywhere. And it is richly endowed with hills and glens and lochs and rivers that thrilled my angling heart.

But, sadly, we found in this beautiful part of the *Country of the Book* very little evangelical enthusiasm. There are exceptions – a number of brave brothers and sisters here and there who are praying for a revival and striving untiringly towards that end. Donald King, postmaster of Wigtown, is one of them. American-born, he came to Ulster in quest of adventure in 1957, and was so impressed with the Province that he decided to remain for a further period. Then he met and married Nesta, a schoolteacher, and successfully applied for British citizenship.

Mr and Mrs King, who have two daughters, Charlotte Anne and Jennifer, had a lucrative dry-cleaning business in South Armagh, but the troubles there made them part with it in favour of the quietude of Wigtown, where they are closely associated with the local Baptist outreach.

Donald, and his butcher friend Sandy and company, were instrumental in organising a Saturday evenng Praise and Music Rally in Wigtown County Hall, which Victor and I conducted. Our efforts were rewarded with a number of people remaining behind in a bid to find lasting peace. Then I had the pleasure and honour of returning to the same hall to take part in a special Evening of Praise to commemorate the Centenary of the Wigtown Martyrs – an occasion which had a wonderful feeling of spiritual revival, for seldom was a larger crowd seen gathered locally to listen to music and a Gospel message.

On the Saturday afternoon prior to that memorable evening in the County Hall, Wigtown was packed with visitors for the Martyrs Memorial Service in the graveyard, where the remains of the two brave women lie. As I strolled around town I figured I was the only Ulsterman present. But the surprise of a lifetime was in store, for the speaker at the open-air service was the Revd. Professor Edward Donnelly, of the New Testament Theological Hall, Belfast, and minister of Newtownabbey Reformed Presbyterian Church, and the very able presenter was the Revd. Dr Hugh Blair, minister of Ballymoney Reformed Presbyterian Church. Both gentlemen are friends of mine. When Dr Blair led the Psalm-singing I further discovered that the voices of Ballyclabber Reformed Presbyterian Church Choir were also in full force – and how lovely and harmonious they sounded! An essence of pride filled my heart for my fellow countrymen and women, for their contributuion to this historic event. It would be fitting at this juncture to include a short history of the Martyrs.

It was in the seventeenth century that King Charles tried to reintroduce Bishops and Episcopacy into the Scottish Presbyterian Church. An act had been passed, known as the Test Act, which required subjects to swear an oath of loyalty to the King, recognising him as head of the church.

It was this 'Test' that Margaret McLachlan, aged sixty-three, and Margaret Wilson, eighteen, could not and did not assent to.

Margaret Wilson was the eldest daughter of Gilbert

Wilson, a yeoman of Penninghame, Wigtownshire. Born at Glenverock in 1667, she retained her Presbyterian faith, although her parents, probably for their own personal safety, had conformed to Episcopalianism. Margaret and her thirteen-year-old sister Agnes were instructed to conform to Episcopalian teaching, but said 'No'.

On April 18th, 1685, Margaret Wilson, Agnes Wilson and Margaret McLachlan were put on trial at Wigtown Assizes before the sheriff depute, David Graham, and three other judges. The charges against them were rebellion and attendance of field conventicles – services held in defiance of the law.

Each of the three refused to swear the oath of abduration, which would have meant promising to give up their allegiance to Presbyterianism.

The girls and woman held their heads high as they were sentenced to be tied to the stakes, which the water of Bladnoch flowed over. They were to be drowned by the incoming tide.

Later it was agreed to release the child, Agnes Wilson, when her father bailed her on a bond of £100 – a lot of money then. The other two women were taken to the place of execution under heavy guard. They were watched by a large sullen crowd, and there was much weeping.

The older woman's stake was a fair distance beyond the other, and her fate was obviously intended to force the younger Margaret to change her mind. After Margaret McLachlan was dead, and the water was creeping up Margaret Wilson's chest, she was given another chance to renounce her Presbyterianism, and to take the oath. But she refused, and passed on into glory with the Twenty-fifth Psalm ringing in her ears.

The victims of the 1685 repression are remembered by a stone put at the place of execution, an inscribed slate tablet in the graveyard, and an imposing Windy Hill Covenanter Memorial, which tourists flock to see.

It was a gratifying experience being a small part of the services exactly three hundred years later, when the two Margarets were solemnly remembered for their uncompromising faith, love and obedience to the King of Kings. Indeed, when the younger Margaret was asked by a soldier to study the plight of the older woman she replied: 'What do I see but Christ wrestling out yonder!'

On the outskirts of Wigtown is Bladnoch Village, which has two claims to recognition, both based on 'liquid assets' – a creamery and a distillery. I had to pass through this village to get to Kirwaugh Farm, a vast dairy project operated by yet another Ulsterman, Jack Robinson, and oh, what a welcome I received!

Jack and his wife Lesley, since coming to Wigtown in 1976, have become popular and industrious members of the community. The genial couple had a family of eight – Ian, Denise, David, Elizabeth, Steven, Gail, Andrew and Mark. But one morning, Denise, just nineteen and a university student with a promising academic career, died. We who knew and loved her were shocked and saddened. My answer to the sudden and untimely passing is that God wanted an angel and called on Denise. She was a gem and an exemplary Christian.

Shortly afterwards Lesley and Jack had the gift of another baby daughter, Gillian, and we all love her.

The Robinson household was a busy one, with reveille sounding loud and clear at 5 am. The eligible members of the family had to do their respective jobs in the up-to-date milking parlour, which housed more than two hundred cows. And that was a spectacle to behold! Milking over, each junior worker had a shower, then dressed in a smart school uniform, sat down to breakfast. But no one lifted a knife, fork or spoon until dad read a portion of scripture and thanked God for His provision.

A few days' stay at the Robinson home is a wonderfully

exhilirating experience, for apart from dedicated Christian fellowship and the excellent food Lesley cooks (with no regard for calories), a salmon and trout river meanders through the 350 acre farm, which for me makes it a veritable paradise.

Mrs Mona Stewart resides in the fine town of Newton Stewart, Wigtownshire, with her gamekeeper husband, Bobbie.

Formerly known as 'Galloway's Queen of Song', this gifted lady has toured America and Canada and appeared in major theatres as a singer of Scottish ballads. Her soprano voice is very special. But away from the bright lights Mona is quiet and modest, and was often tagged 'the ideal house-wife'. Her chief interest was her family and home, and Bobbie and she gave little thought to matters of religion.

But some years ago, Fay, their youngest daughter, went to study at Glasgow University and was fortunate to meet a number of Christian students who influenced her to join them on that road to a better and brighter land. Fay's parents were in bed the night she rang to convey the good news of her conversion. Mona had answered the phone, and she wasn't quite sure what her daughter was talking about, especially when Fay said she would have to break off with her non-Christian boyfriend. But she was quick to detect that the voice on the line was emphatic and happy.

Back in bed, Mona told Bobbie what she had just heard. His sleepy reply was: 'Well, sure it's better than getting drunk.'

Next morning Fay phoned her boyfriend whose parents were Christians, and after explaining about her commitment to Christ she added: 'I wish to remain a good friend, but I feel in my heart that the courtship must finish.' She was in for a surprise! Her boyfriend, the parents told her, had accepted Christ at exactly the same time she had on the previous day. Soon the young couple were walking closely with God together, and everything was well.

Their supreme happiness impressed Mona and she began thinking. One evening at home, prior to leaving to keep a cabaret date, she was compelled to open a Bible and read, on Fay's request, John 3:16. So deeply was she touched and convicted that she couldn't do the cabaret spot, in spite of the pleading phone calls.

Mona began singing for the Lord, and six months after her conversion, her husband Bobbie joined her in Christian faith. This encouraged the other members of the family to follow in their footsteps. Today they are all trophies of grace. I myself have much pleasure and joy working with Mona from time to time, in Scotland and Ireland.

Victor Hutchinson and I spent a really super touring holiday in the company of Mr and Mrs William Millar or Dumfries.

Like the Robinsons, they are Ulster folk, and are engaged in dairy farming with a prime Friesian herd. Rhys Farm is quite isolated, but this does not deter Mr and Mrs Millar from preparing their spacious sitting room and having times of fellowship, to which they invite people from miles around. There can never be any excuses about not having transport, for big William always has the Land Rover and car on duty and, if necessary, the tractor!

We had inspiring morning and evening meetings in the Millar home. As the singing and music went out of the open windows and echoed across the picturesque countryside we prayed that if any folk had stayed away they would be blessed by the sound and encouraged to come to the next get-together.

William Millar is an earnest worker for the Lord, and when he was informed that Victor and I were coming to Dumfries he booked the community hall and so threw us straight into the fray. To our pleasant surprise there was a large turn-out, thanks to our host's prayer and publicity stunts, and, of course, to the Land Rover and car.

Two men sat smoking. They gave me the notion they were present for the sole purpose of seeing a couple of hours of music-hall. But Mona Stewart on piano, Victor on his giant electronic accordion, and myself on saxophone set the rally going. In a matter of seconds the members of the audience were clapping their hands and singing with gusto *This Is The Day That The Lord Hath Made*. The cigarette smoke was no more to be seen!

The Holy Spirit, as usual, was present and Victor brought a great rally to a close with a challenging message. I made a point of speaking to the two smokers and learned that they were father and son. They had come along to please the mother, who was a Christian, and most concerned about their heavy drinking. As I took the offered hand of the older man, he said in all sincerity: 'We have been taught a lot tonight . . . we are certainly glad we came.' And so was I, even though they did have a wee smoke.

William Millar had some prison work lined up for me. It was most rewarding. I would like to go into details, but I'm afraid that I was obliged as a journalist to promise not to write anything on the activities inside, and I have to stand my my word. On the last morning of our stay, William invited us to the home of Keith Sinclair, which overlooks a magnificent panorama of ocean and is used extensively in the service of the Lord.

We felt we knew Keith before we met him, for brother William had spoken in glowing terms of his work and his sterling Christian qualities. In that elevated mansion we enjoyed real Scottish warmth and hospitality, and received golden evidence of the virtues William extolled.

Chapter Nine

On one cross-Channel tour, Victor and I had wonderfully fruitful meetings in several towns, including Stranraer, Paisley, Ayr, Peterhead, Dumfries, Falkirk, Dunfermline and Carlisle. What encouragement it was seeing sinners step forward in response to our appeals and kneel at the foot of the Cross! We journeyed to the different venues in a van that had seen better days. But the Lord always got us there in one piece and in time. Once again, we didn't have to pay a penny for accommodation. There were always people offering us a place in their homes. We were overwhelmed with kindness.

In Falkirk I enjoyed the hospitality of Mr and Mrs Charlie Ramsey. Mary, Charlie's wife, is a great cook. I never will forget her special bread with cheese and pineapple toasted into it. I brought the simple receipe back to Ireland, and today many housewives here are finding it an economical and time-saving family favourite.

The town of Falkirk was not strange to me. Oh no, and my visit refreshed a lot of wartime memories. Falkirk is associated with the strangest coincidence of my life. Let me tell you about it.

In the dark days of 1940 I was based in Falkirk's neighbouring town, Grangemouth, in an anti-aircraft battery, guarding hundreds of giant oil tanks from enemy air strikes. It was a rather precarious assignment.

One afternoon near Christmas, Battery Lieutenant Brian Clark and I were shown around the historic Calander

House in Falkirk by the housekeeper, Miss Haddow. The owners, Mr and Mrs Forbes, were absent on war work in England. The first room we entered was once occupied by Bonnie Prince Charlie, whose letters are framed and displayed on the walls. Miss Haddow then directed us through a long corridor, whose carpents alone would have cost a fortune, to a magnificent staircase often used by Oliver Cromwell. Another set of rooms was complete with beds and bedclothes and a plaque inscribed: 'These rooms were slept in by Mary, Queen of Scots, and her ladies, 1652-1656.' Miss Haddow explained that Queen Victoria had visited the house on a number of occasions during her long reign, and that the present lady of the house, Mrs Forbes, was a direct descendant of Oliver Cromwell.

I wrote an article on Calandar House in an Irish paper, the *Northern Constitution*, and sent Miss Haddow a copy. I still have her appreciative reply in my chest of treasures.

When I changed my khaki for the blue of the Royal Air Force, I was posted to the 57 Operational Training Unit, situated twenty-five miles from Newcastle-Upon-Tyne. One Bank Holiday when no buses were running I was hitch-hiking to Newcastle, when the lady driver of a small Fire Service van picked me up. The lady was dressed in a blue uniform. Beside her sat a gentleman in civilian clothes whom, I later learned, was her husband.

During the journey I explained that I had served in Scotland, prior to my transfer into the RAF.

'Which part of Scotland?' the lady asked.

'Grangemouth,' I replied.

'Wonderful,' the lady said. 'My husband and I live near to Grangmouth. Our home is in Falkirk.'

'Falkirk!' I exclaimed, 'I was intrigued with a visit to the famous Calandar House there.'

'That is our home,' came the reply.

My two companions were Mr and Mrs Forbes. I could

hardly speak with surprise! When we arrived in Newcastle, the charming couple invited me into a big black-stone terraced house, entertained me with coffee, and showed me my article on Calandar House which Miss Haddow had sent them. Stranger than fiction, isn't it?

When in Dunfermline, I stayed in the Presbyterian Manse with the Revd. Charles Cameron, and his homely wife Sharon. Charles is minister of a very fine church in town. It has its own newspaper which is not backward about giving non-attending members a polite telling off.

Mrs Cameron hails from Ballymoney. The good lady, after committing herself to Christ, joined the Faith Mission and on completing her time of study successfully at Edinburgh Bible College, was appointed assistant in the Faith Mission book Shop, Dunfermline, under Superintendent Sandy Moyan. This is where Cupid and his bow slip romantically into the story. One fine day during a sales period, Charles, the young clergyman, entered the Faith Mission Book Shop hunting for a bargain and got Sharon, the Irish colleen. The couple were married in Drumreagh Presbyterian Church, County Antrim, by the Revd. Tom Luke, who helped me considerably in the initial stages of my Christian walk.

As I thanked Mr and Mrs Cameron for looking after me so well, Charles conceded a burning desire. Said he: 'I will be forever grateful to Tom Luke for tying a very happy and tight knot for Sharon and I. In sweet reciprocation I would cherish the job of crossing to Ireland and tying a happy and tight knot for Tom, when his turn comes.'

I am also pleased to have worked with the Revd. James Luke, Tom's brother, who is the esteemed minister of Dungiven Presbyterian Church, County Londonderry. The father of James and Tom Luke, the late Archie Luke, a Battle of the Somme hero, was pleased when his sons became skilled tradesmen in their native town of Ahoghill. But the Lord wanted the lads in His service, and He called them. James' first church was Carnlough on the rugged Antrim coast, where he had the unique idea of making his harvest-thanksgiving service a maritime one, with the pulpit transformed into the prow of a ship – most appropriate as many of his flock were fishermen.

At the moment of writing James and Tom have the distinction of being area moderators of the Presbyterian Church in Ireland. The evangelical brothers have pointed numerous sinners to the Lord in the course of their ministries.

I used to think that northern England was a bleak place, with a profusion of coalmines and slag heaps. I was wrong. During my wartime spell in Northumberland and Cumberland, I got to know of their agricultural importance. From road, rail or air could be seen miles and miles of fertile soil and splendid crops. My rambles from Tynemouth to Carlisle have rewarded me with some of the most interesting sight-seeing tours I have ever undertaken – rugged coastal scenery that contrasted picturesquely with brown and purple hills and green valleys. But the farming and the region's wild beauty are not the only attractions. My attention was further drawn to the relics of a unique history, one spectacular feat of which is Hadrian's Wall, stretching from Newcastle to Carlisle, and acclaimed as the finest Roman antiquity in Britain. This immense defence shield was built over fifteen hundred years before the invention of steam.

So as Victor and I entered Carlisle in our old van to conduct a Praise Rally, it was not strange to me, although forty-three years had passed since I was last there.

How could I ever describe the atmosphere in the Elim Free Church that evening? I am completely lost for words.

From start to finish the Holy Spirit took full control and we could do nothing wrong. Under His powerful influence the music, the singing, the testimony and the message went faultlessly.

A dear sister wept throughout the Rally, and when I spoke to her at the end she gave a sad reason for the flow of tears. Her mother, who had cancer, played Victor Hutchinson's record *Heaven Is Nearer Since Mother Is There* during the course of her illness, and was actually listening to it as she passed into that brighter land.

One little girl of twelve was so convicted on the evening of the Rally that she could not sleep. After tossing and turning in distress whe called on her Christian daddy to point her to the Lord, and peace and sleep immediately came to her.

The pastor of the Carlisle Free Elim Church is Sydney Reid. I am pleased to say that he is Ulster-born, and the father of the noted Gospel recording singer, Sharon Reid, now married to Paul Gardener, also a gifted musician and singer for the Lord. I meet this young couple at Praise Services in all parts of the Province and it is a real joy to chat and have fellowship with them.

Our hosts in Carlisle were Tommy and Chrissie McGlade and they looked after us lavishly.

Tommy McGlade is an extraordinary fellow. I know of no one in England, Scotland, Wales and Ireland who travels more than he does. His last car registered an amazing 82,000 miles in less than two years. And all the time he is witnessing mightily for the Lord as a sales representative for a Christian literature firm. A native of Cookstown, County Tyrone, the 'broth o' a bouy' entered the Faith Christian Mission Movement, and through initiative and dedication rose high in the ranks prior to accepting his present position.

It was while serving in the Faith Mission that Tommy

met Chrissie, a pretty lassie from the Isle of Skye, and soon wedding bells were ringing for the pair of pilgrims, who provided the perfect match for each other. Now they are blessed with two bonnie children, Alan and Lindsay, and the evidence of the family's happiness radiates throughout their comfortable home.

We left Carlisle, very much impressed with the kindness of Pastor Reid, his really wonderful assembly, and with the hospitality of Tommy and Chrissie. Then it was back on the road to dear old Scotland again, our destination being Dumfries Methodist Church, where we received a warm welcome and losts of encouragement from the large congregation.

An alcoholic, in an intoxicated state, was present at the meeting, and he asked to see me during the interval. I agreed, and followed him into a counselling room – but not with the same enthusiasm as the stewards have on saving someone's soul. No man who is 'lit up' with the devil's oil has the wits to discuss his future. Always beware of the cunning streak in a person who craves drink. He will do anything to get it!

I was not surprised when the unfortunate creature produced a cheque book and asked me 'in the name of God' to cash a cheque, as the hotel around the corner wouldn't take one. The alternative if I didn't oblige, he stressed, was a night lying out in the cold. I gave him £7 of loose change I had in my pocket, for which he handed me a scribbled cheque and then left the church in a hurry – probably hunting for the first pub. When the cheque bounced higher than a rubber ball I wasn't surprised, having used similar seedy methods myself as I stood shaking in desperation for that 'life-saving' drink. I only trust and pray that the addicted rogue accepts my sound advice and gets on the right road before it is too late.

The final meeting of our tour was in Stranraer, the venue

being a handsome old church with excellent acoustics – a welcome bonus to musicians. The large number of folk present included a bus load of our friends from Wigtown. Two days later, Donald King, the bus organiser, rang me in Ireland to say that on arrival at Wigtown one of their party, a lad with a lot of worldly problems, approached the local Baptist pastor, and before going home committed himself to Christ Jesus. Victor and I rejoiced at the news and again thanked God for such great results from our humble efforts in His service.

Shortly after my homecoming, I booked the Portstewart Town Hall for a Stauros Foundation Rally of praise, testimony, music and song, and there was a great attendance response. The dynamic Pastor Arthur Williams, founder of Stauros, led the meeting, while I looked after the music. The principal speaker was the Revd. Ron Baker, from Australia, who confided that at the age of thirty he could neither read nor write and had an embarrassing speech impediment. In addition he had been a chronic alcoholic, and a drug addict of the worst possible type. But through the mercy of God the afflicted man was forced to attend a Billy Graham Campaign in the city of Sydney in 1959. His wife Beryl had been converted at a previous meeting, and though none expected him to follow he made a profession, and full happiness entered into the Baker home.

For three years the young Christian had to have the Bible read to him. So engrossed did he become in the scriptures that he decided to go to school to learn how to read it himself. At the same time he underwent speech therapy, and eventually the wonderful day came when he qualified to study for the Baptist ministry in a Bible College. Ron paid his college fees by driving a bus in his spare hours. When his transport colleagues heard of his successful graduation they presented him with theological books worth $1,000. Since then Ron Baker has travelled all over Australia helping alcoholics and all kinds of problematic people.

By now you will gather it didn't take me long as a Christian to take on new committments. It meant me moving fast each week to get a human-interest page together for the paper. But with my permanent sobriety, renewed vigour and a number of faithful scouts tipping me off about potential subjects, I accepted the challenge with confidence.

It was on a Monday morning that I heard of Robin McNaul. This young man's phone, in his Coleraine Music Centre, could have rung at any minute of the day with a request for his services to back a recording group, a solo singer, a concert ensemble, a travelling Hillbilly outfit, or a full orchestra. Robin is a guitarist of top quality, and in that capacity he travelled widely, leaving his business in the hands of a competent manager.

I once fished salmon on the upper river Bann and on the morning I fulfilled my interviewing appointment in the Music Centre, I did not recognise Robin as the boy who rowed his late dad's boat on the same stretch. He, in fact, mentioned this and I was delighted, for I knew his dad well. I also learned that in the days of his youth, not so long ago, Robin decided to make angling a 'second best', and develop the natural love he had for music. And what better place could he find for study than the home overlooking the river?

Robin, like many beginners on guitar, didn't have the notion to play a tune in a hurry. With the aid of a simple tutor, he took it slowly a step at a time, and also went in search of ideas from more experienced guitarists. He made it to the top. The patience and determination with which he achieved success, he attributes to the boyhood years he spent angling.

The article on Robin's musical ability appeared as the lead story in my page, and was well received by the paper's large readership. A firm friendship had now been established between us, and as I frequented his Music Centre I spoke of the joy and the security of being a Christian. We actually played the songs of Zion together on our instruments. I couldn't help thinking what a great witness Robin would be for the Lord, with his music and lovely disposition. But never once had I put the question of Salvation to him, knowing of interest in dance band and show circles, which was making him money. Instead, I added him to my prayer list.

Readers can envisage the tremendous joy that overwhelmed me one morning in the Music Centre when Robin said: 'My fiance and I met your wonderful friend Jesus yesterday evening and accepted him into our hearts, and we are very, very happy.'

Today, Robin McNaul still travels widely to play guitar, but solely for the Lord. He is lead guitarist in the forty-piece *Youth Mix* orchestra, which is contributing much towards the religious revival we can sense coming to Northern Ireland. God speed it on!

Chapter Ten

Victor Hutchinson and I had invitations to conduct Praise Rallies in a number of distant spots, such as Shetland, Orkney and the Outer and Inner Hebrides. Usually we could not accept them owing to our limited spare time and the antiquated road system. But the exuberant Victor, ever keen to serve the Lord, came to me one morning and asked: 'Do you like flying?'

'No,' I returned, 'it makes my arms ache.'

'Seriously,' he said, 'a friend of mine, Michael Kirk, has a small aeroplane. He is going to fly us to those far-away places, with the Lord as his co-pilot . . . will you come?'

I agreed, and so it was with some excitement that the three of us, plus instruments, left a derelict airfield in the north west of Ireland, for Fort William in the Highlands of Scotland.

We had a clear beautiful view of our native land. There, on the left was the Giant's Causeway with its neat hexagonal formations, said to be the world's eighth wonder. Many theories have been published regarding its origin, but Alex Martin, the 'King of the Causeway', who sells his personally-made blackthorn walking sticks, shillelaghs and minature causeway stones to tourists from all over the world, favours the Giant Theory in preference to all others. He begins by giving an account of the origin of the name Giant's Causeway, in an elaborate and picturesque version of the mythical legend that the great causeway was the commencement of a road across the Channel to Scotland, in order that a fight should take place between Finn MacCool, the Irish giant, and the Scottish giant.

To our right lay dear old Ballycastle on the North Antrim coast, and out in the broad ocean directly opposite was Rathlin Island. Guglielmo Marconi had a close association with both places during his early radio experiments. It was in September 1898 that the Italian genius and his right-hand man, George Kemp, first demonstrated wireless telegraphy, between Rathlin and Ballycastle, a distance of eight miles.

Romantic Rathlin was where King Robert the Bruce once lived in exile. Most of us are familiar with the legend of the king being attracted by the efforts of a spider to reach its web at the top of the cave in which he was hiding. At the seventh attempt the spider succeeded, so Bruce was encouraged to slip back to Scotland, reform his armies and engage the English in battle again. He gained victory at Bannockburn, and ultimately secured Scottish independence.

Some years ago I visited Rathlin, in a journalistic capacity, in the company of Lord Bruce, a descendant of the Royal Bruces of Scotland. He had with him the gallant King Robert's sword and, in a small glass jar, the monarch's teeth, which were excavated from his tomb.

The Rathlin Islanders are known as Raghery folk and they are an exemplary community with all denominations living in peaceful harmony. If the Roman Catholic chapel is in need of repair, the congregation is invited to worship in the little Protestant church, and vice-versa.

Flying certainly proved to be fast, economical and convenient. One hour and thirty-five minutes after leaving Ireland, Michael landed perfectly at Oban Airport, and we were on our way by car to fulfil an engagement in the Fort William Faith Mission Hall – another meeting we will always remember for the blessing we received.

Victor and I have got special books printed that contain a good and lively selection of choruses. When my partner starts leading them on that giant electronic accordion, which can imitate every musical instrument from the Hammond organ to the jew's harp, he really gets people going. But, alas, we do not always attract big crowds. We once arrived at a Highland village hall to find only one man present – not a very encouraging start to a meeting that had been well advertised.

As Victor mounted his equipment and speakers I whispered: 'Surely we're not going to play for one man?'

'Speedy,' he replied, 'that man, in turning up, has been loyal to you and to me, so he is going to get the full programme . . . go down and tell him.'

I went to the man sitting in the middle of the hall and said: 'Thank you, sir, for coming. Mr Hutchinson told me to tell you that for your loyalty you are going to get the full programme.'

'Well, you'd better get on with it,' said the man. 'I've got to lock up!'

As its name suggests, Fort William was formerly a military settlement built in 1654 by General Monk, to keep the rumbustious Highland clans in check. Four and a half miles south of it lies Britain's highest mountain, Ben Nevis. Mountains fascinate me. From boyhood it has been my ambition to climb one. But as I scanned the dizzy heights of bold Ben Nevis I decided once and for all to abandon my ambitions and leave it to the mountaineers.

Next day we flew south to Portpatrick, to provide music at the wedding reception of a brethren couple. They had booked the Knockinaam Lodge Hotel, situated on the rugged coast of this little known and unspoiled corner of Scotland. Quaint villages, early Christian monuments, ruined and still inhabited castles dot an undulating green landscape. Such was the timelessness and tranquillity of

99

this place that Sir Winston Churchill chose it during the Second World War for a secret meeting with General Eisenhower and their Chiefs of Staff.

The marriage we were invited to had united a charming Scottish widow and a rollicking Irish widower, and they and their hundred guests certainly showed their apprication of our hymnal selections by joining in and really praising God.

But soon we were airborne again, headed this time for the Isle of Skye, a popular holiday resort that is usually reached by the way of Kyle of Lochalsh, and the ferry to the pleasant village of Kyleaking. We landed at the small airport just in time to beat a belt of rough rainy weather, which was coming in fast from the north.

Kyleakin was our head-quarters. We were the guests of Mr and Mrs Callum McAskill, who served the food in true Hebridean style – fresh, hot and plentiful. Callum's wife, Margaret, who comes from the north of the island, speaks fluent Gaelic. Indeed, she learned the native language before learning English. They have four pretty daughters, Catriona, Mairi, Christine, and Ruth.

Callum was joint-organiser of our meeting in the Parish Church hall, Portree, and as he transported us there, he gave an informative commentary on our surroundings. The complex rock formations of Skye, like the Giant's Causeway, are of particular interest to students of geology. Three quarters of its surface is covered with solidified lava. This enchanting island has a number of smaller islands close to its coasts. On the west side are Wiay, Soay, Canna, Rum and Eigg. On the east side are Rona, Raasay, Scalpay and Pabay. If it is God's will, I'll return and explore them.

Portree, the capital of Skye, has a population of 1,500. The Revd. John Ferguson, minister of the local Parish Church, kindly chaired the evening of praise, and Victor and I were very impressed with the singing both of his flock and folk of other denominations. The church hall reverberated with the joyous sound. So much so that we wondered if living an unpolluted life by the sea had anything to do with the splendid voices that rang out so clearly and sweetly.

Our flight to the Island of Benbecula in the Outer Hebrides was less pleasant. We had nosed into thick mist and cloud and could see nothing but ourselves in the small compartment overlooking the wings. The constant purr of the engine made conversation difficult, so I spent most of the journey alone with my thoughts. There is no place more thought-provoking than the middle of a cloud!

Michael landed with the aid of instruments and runway lights. Understandably, we found waiting for us two fire engines, and an airport controller who reckoned we should not have been flying on such a day. But the Benbecula Baptist assembly had looked forward to our visit for a long time, and would have been greatly disappointed if we had not got there.

What was my first impression of the island? A bleak one, I'm afraid. The dreary sky, the rain and grey mist combined to make the place not too heartsome. But believe me, things warmed up when we met Cecil Collins, who had come with a van to take us to his home at Aird. His accent instantly proclaimed him a native of dear old Belfast, and every word he spoke sounded like a breath of home.

A civil engineer by profession, Cecil is in charge of the building of a large boarding school in Benbecular. Such is its isolation that the pupils will not be wooed by the bright lights and pleasures of the world! Cecil and his wife, Elaine, and children Claire, Peter and Andrew, have settled in a comfortable bungalow and will remain there until the school is in use. They have been well received in the local community.

After a four-course dinner we were taken down to the

101

Baptist musical evening. The large attendance included Army and RAF families from the military base. And oh what a joy it was to learn that the Holy Spirit is moving as freely there as in other parts of the island. The liberty we experienced was marvellous.

The next morning we were promptly served an Ulster-fry breakfast and then directed round the island by Elaine. Though it is only ten miles in circumference, there is much to see among Benbecula's numerous trout-stocked lakes and costal scenery. According to legend a missionary named St Torran had been on his way to Ireland to evangelise, but he got lost and his craft was eventually blown on to the shore at Benbecular. He anchored, and built a church of stones in the sacred name of the Irish saint Columba. It still stands to this day.

I am told that the island's history compares with anything in the Hebridean group. During the centuries of invasions and clan feuds it provided shelter for the fugitive Bonnie Prince Charlie and his supporters in 1746. The beloved prince escaped the net of the English redcoats by posing as Flora MacDonald's Irish servant, Betty Burke. His Royal Highness played the part well!

We stopped and surveyed the smallest church in the entire Outer and Inner Islands, which opens for services each Sunday under the ministry of the Church of Scotland, and has the distinction of having received informal visits from Queen Elizabeth.

It was just wonderful meeting the people of Benbecula, and joining them in fellowship. We took off in the afternoon for Inverness on the Scottish mainland, but before setting course, Michael did a couple of farewell flights low around the island in a tricky aeronautical manoeuvre of thanks. The waving of arms and handkerchiefs from beneath showed that our friends had got the message. That particualar afternoon was ideal for flying.

To avoid coming in contact with high hills and mountains we went up to 5,000 feet. It was like a fairyland above the snow-white pearly clouds. It seemed as if we could step out of the cabin and walk on them.

Inverness has an attractive situation, with the River Ness flowing through its centre. The history of the Scottish city goes back to the dark ages. Recent archaeological excavations have revealed much of the prehistory of the area. A timber structure proved that a domestic habitation existed in the Mesolithic era around 5,000 BC, so that's going back quite a bit.

I found the Inverness community warm and hospitable just like the folk in other Scottish towns, and in the homes we visited the kettle was always on the boil. On the evening of our arrival we presented a musical programme in the local Baptist Church, in front of a large congregation and video cameras. Every face was welcoming and happy, and gave us the feeling we had known them for years. Even before we spoke a word, or played a note on our instruments, we knew we were going to have a great time of praise. The full glorifying of God that followed was really indescribable.

The esteemed pastor of Inverness Baptist Church is none other than the Revd. William Freel, renowned exponent of the Scriptures, and one of the distinguished speakers at the Irish Portstewart Convention each summer. During our visit to his church, Mr Freel was preaching in Lurgan, County Armagh, but it was our good fortune to meet Betty, his charming wife, who, with Angus and Mairi Morrison of the Faith Mission, gave us every encouragement. Angus and Mairi were our hosts.

At Inverness Tourist Information Office next morning I was interested to read in a booklet the leading and courageous part Angus Og MacDonald played in the battle of Bannockburn in 1314. This warrior was fostered by the O'Cahan Clan of Dungiven, Northern Ireland, and on reaching manhood he married the beautiful Finvola O'Cahan, and took her to his native Islay in Scotland. But some years later, Finvola died and her remains were brought back to Dungiven and buried at the old Priory Church there. Toal O'Cahan, the clan bard, lay weeping by Finvola's bier and didn't leave it until he composed the elegy, *Finvola, The Gem of The Roe*. The Roe, of course, is a beautiful river that rises in the Sperrin Mountains and flows through the towns of Dungiven and Limavady. The Finvola elegy is still sung with feeling around the hearthstones of Irish farmsteads.

It goes like this:

> In the land of O'Cahan, where bleak
>   mountains rise,
> O'er whose brown, ridgy tops now the
>   dusky cloud flies;
> Deep sunk in a valley a wild flower
>   did grow
> And her name was Finvola, the Gem of
>   the Roe.
>
> From the Island of Islay appeared to our
>   view
> A youth clad in tartan, as strange as
>   'tis true,
> With a star on his breast, and unstrung
>   was his bow,
> And he sighed for Finvola, the Gem of
>   the Roe.
>
> No more up the streamlet her maidens
>   shall hie,

For wan the cold cheek and bedimm'd
  the blue eye;
In silent affliction our sorrows shall
  flow
Since gone is Finvola, the Gem of the
  Roe.

Chapter Eleven

I would never wish to hear it said in my company that the Aberdonian is a hard, miserable man who carries his purse in his left pocket and tries to reach it with the right hand. No, no, no – nothing could be further from the truth.

During a series of meetings we were taking in North East Scotland, our guide and driver was Aberdeen-born Ali Boyd, a retired ship's engineer and a pillar of Boddam Evangelical Church. This kind Christian brother would let Victor and I spend nothing, and in getting us to the venues he showed outstanding efficiency – with one exception when he drove at speed up a one-way street, in spite of the shouting, sounding of horns and flashing headlights by those motorists going in the other direction. But we eventually reached our destination, Northsound Radio Station, to do a recording for the Scottish *Sunday Best* programme. Everything went well, thanks to the producer-presenter, Gill Poole.

Ali and I spent an interesting hour in the Sunnybrae Christian Centre, chatting with a number of alcoholics who were being treated there. Most of them had the usual story to tell about marriage break-up, the wrecking of a home, the suffering of children, the loss of a fortune, and the final, total despair. They were making efforts to beat the curse, and finding lots of support from the energetic super-intendent, Norman Ogston. Prior to leaving I prescribd a definite cure for the horrible disease of chronic alcoholism that costs not a single penny. Victims can achieve this by simply putting their trust in God and praying for the touch of His healing hand, His love and His comfort. I am living proof of this.

Ali, who has sailed the seven seas and witnessed the depravity of the world, spoke a moving wee word and gave sound advice, which Norman and I heartily endorsed. We feel that the visit was a rewarding one.

Boddam is situated forty miles north of Aberdeen, and the development of the North Sea has changed it from a small fishing village to a nerve centre of the world oil business. The harbour that once sheltered part of the coast's fishing fleet is now given over entirely to the servicing and supply of mighty oil-rigs.

Our hosts in Boddam were Mr and Mrs Alex Duthie. Alex is one of the founder elders of the Boddam Evangelical Church, which is just across the road from his home. His wife Nan is church organist. The lively church has seven other elders who, like Alex, do tremendous work without regard for personal inconvenience. Apart from their own packed Praise Rally, which Victor and I led, they had organised others in the Peterhead Auditorium, Torry United Free Church, Aberdeen, Gardenstown Parish Church, Buckie Fishermens Hall, and the Peterhead Assemblies of God Church. We enjoyed taking part in every one of them. Yes, those elders are truly men of God, and He is richly blessing their efforts.

Alex and Nan Duthie's comfortable home is named 'Stqsanden', hope you can get your tongue round it, for mine failed hopelessly. Our initial meal was most fitting to the martitime surroundings – a variety of delicious fresh fish. Seated beside me at the top of the table was Nan's father, Robert Bruce, and what a wonderful old gentleman he is. It is said along Scotland's east coat that Robert has wrung more salt water out of his socks than many a young sailor has sailed upon. He went to sea at the age of fourteen and did not retire until he was past seventy-six – a record of sixty-two years, many of them spent as skipper.

In the old days Robert sailed from Aberdeen to the Arctic Circle, and every spare minute, as a devout Christian, he turned to his Bible. He encouraged his crew to do the same. As we conversed I lent an ear to a nice wee human-interest story about Robert's uncle, who was also a skipper and a Christian.

Uncle, when at sea, always made a point of getting to the Port of Baag, in the Faroe Islands, so he could take a Sunday morning service in the local church. The islanders always looked forward to him coming, for he could really expound the word!

In that era the Faroe folk depended greatly on whale meat for their winter food, and one particular year, when the giant mammals were scarce, there was widespread concern. Then on a certain Sunday morning while Uncle's ship was berthed in the harbour a shoal of whales came inshore, and so he sent this message: 'There'll be no Sunday this Lord's Day . . . He's sent us the whales. Alleluia!'

'It was a hard life, fishing in my time,' Robert mused. 'The pulling in of the lines with a heavy fish catch was strenuous and painful, but it had to be done.' He held up his hands at my request and I shuddered at the sight. They were twisted, calloused and scarred from pulling in two and three mile-lines with baited hooks a foot apart. Robert's fishing trips generally lasted for three weeks. He had his mishaps – one of which almost proved to be fatal. He was operating off Orkney, when his trawler, *Doonie Braes*, went aground close to the Old Man of Hoy. Mercifully, all aboard got a footing on the rocks and climed a three-hundred foot cliff face to safety – an answer to prayer.

Fishing is still a dangerous occupation. The afternoon I chatted with old Robert, his niece's fisherman husband was lost overboard in a rough sea. So the next time we sit down to a fish meal and offer thanks for its provision, let us also remember the brave men who handle the lines and nets.

In the company of Alex Duthie, I had an exhilarating experience. We visited Crimond, a village of eight hundred, north of Boddam. It gained a prominent place in the world by giving its name to a setting of the 23rd Psalm. Miss Jessie Buchan, officer of the local church, kindly directed us round the ancient edifice, giving an interesting and informative account of its history. The visitors' book resembled a gazetteer. There were names from all parts of Britain and Eire. I was honoured to add mine.

Crimond Church is small but bright, and inside the peace of God possessed me as I followed Jessie. A list of ministers dating from 1560 can be seen in the vestibule. The present building dates from 1812; the ruins of the previous church, dating from pre-Reformation times, stand in the centre of the old churchyard. At the turn of this century the organ and pulpit were installed, along with the stained-glass windows.

On the right is a memorial to the Revd. Alexander Irvine, DD, who was the minister of the church from 1855 until 1884. Mr Irvine's daughter, Jessie Seymore Irvine, was gifted musically and poetically, and was an exemplary Christian. She sang in the church choir, and one day in 1872 was prompted to sit down and compose another tune to suit the inspiring words of the 23rd Psalm. As she scribbled the notes she never realised what sheer bliss her effort would create for people in all walks of life throughout the world. The 23rd Psalm to the tune *Crimond* was chosen by Queen Elizabeth for her wedding, and Sir Hugh Robertson and the famous Glasgow Orpheus Choir did much to popularise it. It is played and sung in all churches, and is continually requested at weddings and funerals. If Jessie Seymour Irvine had lived in the age of copyright, she would be a millionairess over and over again.

Jessie Buchan gave me a copy of the 23rd Psalm, as it was once sung in northern Scottish churches. Here it is penned by one John Moir, or the Bridge of Feugh, long since gone to be with his Maker.

Wha is my shepherd weel I ken,
The Lord Himsel' is He,
He leads whaur the girse is green,
An' burnies quaet that be.

Aft time I fain astray wad gang,
An' wann'r far awa',
He fins me oot, He pit me richt,
An' brings me hame an' a'.

Tho' I pass through the gruesome clough,
Fin I ken He is near,
His muckle crook will me defen',
Sae I hae nocht to fear.

Ilk comfort whilk a sheep could beed,
His thoughtfu' care provides,
Tho' wolves and dogs may prowl aboot
In safety, me, He hides.

His guidness and His mercy baith
Nae doot will bide wi' me,
While foulded on the fields o' time
Or o' eternity.

The Minister of Crimond Church, the Revd. Alexander McGhee, is also responsible for the affairs of the St Fergus Church. This fine reverend gentleman, who has his hands full with a combined flock of 375 families, always finds time to chat with visitors to Crimond.

When I questioned him about the fish on the church tower, he quickly enlightened me. 'In days gone by,' he explained, 'The Scottish Presbyterian faith was not permitted to be openly discussed, so the fish became the symbol with which Christian folk were identified. It was displayed in different forms and had a great response.'

Alex Duthie transported me that evening to two villages, not far from Crimond, and there I learned of strange customs. In the villages of Cairnbulg and Inverallochy, which are separated only by a narrow street, the natives of Cairnbulg sit on the left side of the local church and the Inverallochy folk occupy the right side. I was amazed to see a similar arrangement in the burying ground outside the village.

Victor and I returned to Northern Ireland, and after separating to see to meetings we had been individually booked for, we teamed up yet again and took to the air for a non-stop flight to the Orkneys. The elements were kind to us until we flew over Loch Ness, for Nessie the monster must have erupted at our noisy presence. It was as if she had blown the turbulence through her wide fiery nostrils to toss us about like a paper bag. An Orkney writer described our temporary plight thus: 'On Monday afternoon the Loch Ness monster, mystery of the Scottish Glen, was greatly disturbed and excited when she not only heard, but saw a flying object with Northern Ireland markings behave rather unusually above her. While there was no reporting of any sightings of the monster, the police and legions of startled observers confirmed the presence of the object and three strange creatures for a period of fifteen minutes.'

Our destination was the Island of Westray, twenty-five miles north of Orkney, and just on the three hours, as scheduled, we landed at the local airport – a field on the farm of Jack Scott, a staunch member of the local Baptist

Church in which we were giving a couple of hours music that evening. Jack, a large cine-camera resting on his broad shoulder, captured on film the arrival of 'the object and the three strange creatures'. Then he and his schoolteacher wife Nan extended us a welcome fit for royalty.

Jack Scott represents Westray and Papa West on the Orkney Council. There was a time when this municipal official found it difficult to get to meetings on the main island, so with his own skilled hands he built an excellent and sea-worthy boat. But the twenty-five mile stretch of water separating Westray and Orkney can have its tempestuous spells, so the brave Jack had to think of another plan to get him to the far-away council chambers. Result? He learned to fly, acquired a small four-seater, and he can now take off at 9 am, and be speaking an hour later.

Westray has a population of seven hundred. There is no unemployment. The hospitable islanders make their living from farming and fishing, with lobsters being a lucrative business. Often windswept, like Benbecula, Westray has its own form of rugged beauty. The atmosphere and sea seem free of pollution of any kind; one can feel the pure air invigorating the lungs and inducing the mind to fully understand why so many city-weary people come here on annual summer pilgrimages.

We were entertained to tea by Pastor James Millar and his wife Irene, and all of my plans to diet went out of the window as the delectable steak and kidney pie was piled in front of us. I just couldn't refuse.

I stayed overnight with Mr and Mrs James Drever, who gave me the best room in their home on the sea-shore, and two hot water bottles to bed. James is a deacon in the Baptist Church and his wife Kathleen is always at hand to help in his Christian work in every way. The couple have two children, Colin, fourteen, and Karen, who is eleven. Big James is also the island's special constable. Another lad and he make up the entire police force, but they are seldom called upon to deal with misdemeanours. In fact, the islanders are so honest and agreeable that cars are never locked, nor are starting keys ever removed from ignitions.

I was pleased to meet a fellow townsman on Westray – the Revd. Joseph Creelman. He was educated in a small rural school, Castleroe, and later worked for his farmer father when the family moved to the coast at Portrush. It was then he became associated with the old-established Ballymagarry Mission Hall, which later influenced him to join the Faith Mission and do a course of Bible study at the Edinburgh College. Twenty years ago he entered the ministry of the Scottish United Free Church, and following an initial period at John O'Groats, and a religious education teaching appointment at Kilmarnock Academy, he took charge of Westray United Church.

Joe met his wife Jessie while she was matron of Wick Hospital, and they have one son, Alan, who gives dad a hand out in the church when he comes home on vacation from training as a computer engineer. October 1986 was a momentous time for the good folk of Ballymagarry, and for Joe, when he returned to open and conduct a three-week mission in the hall which held so many memories for him. Now back with his flock on the lonely island outpost, he often looks back on his boyhood days in Castleroe and Portush and concedes to shedding a wee tear now and again.

Our grateful thanks are due to James and Irene Miller, their daughter Christine and son James, for that evening of fellowship in the Baptist Church. Every seat was occupied and the meeting appears in my diary as 'super'.

Next we went to Shetland. I always had the desire to visit and explore Shetland, which I visualised as a lonely place overrun by midget ponies and sheep. There are certainly small and large ponies and sheep, and perpendicular cliffs packed with puffins, guillemots, razor bills and kittiwakes, but there is also a steady flow of traffic on the five hundred miles of road, so I had to revise my expectations.

The main island is wealthy as it handles half of the UK's oil – a staggering 1,000,000 barrels a day – and is thirteenth in the world oil table, ahead of Libya and Iraq. Lerwick is Shetland's capital town and main port, and it has an excellent shopping centre and an admirable museum. Beneath the flag-stone streets runs a network of passages which were used by smugglers centuries ago. We found the shop-keepers most helpful and courteous.

We were the guests of Mr and Mrs Pat Jamieson, who did us proud by seating us down on arrival to a sumptuous chicken dinner. The potatoes reminded me of the big white floury 'Murphys' we grew in Ireland once-upon-a-time.

Pat and Lorna Jamieson are Shetland's leading gospel singers. I could listen to their recordings continually, for the witness and sheer joy they promote in the heart. They have three fine sons – Aubrey, Clive and Trevor who are following closely in mum and dad's musical footsteps. Aubrey plays an acoustic guitar, Clive is making good progress on the cello at school, and Trevor hopes to be a singer like dad one day.

I had a great hour's crack with Pat's eighty-six-year-old mother, Mrs Jemima Jamieson, who was loud in her praises of Ireland. The good lady has been seventeen times to Kilkenny, where her daughter, Bertha, is married to a hardy farmer, Leonard Harper. I cherished every minute of our talk.

Great friends of the Jamieson family are Mr and Mrs Marshall Russell, who have a Christian book shop in Ballymena, County Antrim. Marshall, prior to coming to Ireland, had a job in Shetland, and so from time to time he likes to return there with his Ulster-born wife Martha to renew old acquaintances.

114

Victor, Michael and I were in Shetland for one night, but during that short time we made many friendships, most of them at the record turn-out for our Praise Rally in Lerwick Baptist Church, and as I took the hands of congregation members in a farewell gesture, following the Epilogue, I felt that they were blood brothers and sisters. They were so homely and encouraging that I am taken by a longing to return to Shetland in the near future for a more extended stay, if the Lord wills it.

Next morning, after prayers for protection and guidance, we left Britain's most northerly island and flew in the direction of Orkney at 3,000 feet, a thick haze depriving us of the views we enjoyed on previous trips. On this particular route we crossed over the place in the ocean where the North Sea and the Atlantic meet, further proof of the Creator's might and power. Indeed, taking in the immensity of the scene when the haze evaporated, I felt so small and humble.

In Kirkwell, the principal town of Orkney, I was put in the charge of Jimic Scott and his gracious wife, whose birth an undisclosed number of years ago caused quite some stir. Her Aunt Christine figured the new-born should be named after her, and an Aunt Isobel staked a similar claim, so to save any animosity the bonnie child was baptised Chrisabel.

Jimic, a brother of the aforementioned Jack Scott of Westray, is a dairy farmer in partnership with Chrisabel's brother, George Rendall. But they hope to retire soon and pass the enterprise on to a nephew.

'Reason?' I asked the two fresh-looking Orcadians.

'To keep the money in the family,' spoke up Chrisabel on behalf of her kinsfolk, and there was a glint of humour in her brown Nordic eyes.

In permanent residence with my Kirkwell hosts is Chrisabel's eighty-five-years young father, George Rendall (senior), who makes a mockery of the term 'retirement'. He must be active from dawn to dusk and being an expert angler he keeps nearby families happy by providing luxurious trout meals.

Jimic Scott accompanied me to the Radio Orkney Studios, where I was to be the guest speaker on the *Thought For The Week* programme. The interviewer asked what record I would like played at the finish of my talk. Without hesitation I replied: '*How Great Thou Art.*'

Later, as I listened to the broadcast, my old heart filled with joy and emotion as the golden tenor voice of Sir Harry Secombe sang my request. This was the choice of the radio producer, and he could not have made a better and more appropriate one.

I was instantly reminded of the afternoon I sat sipping coffee in Harry's caravan and engaging him in conversation. He is so remarkably easy to talk to. For a couple of hours we swopped jokes, during which his laughter rose to that famous high-pitched crescendo, as we referred nostalgically to our wartime experiences in uniform.

Then it was time for the pair of us to go in front of the TV cameras for the Sunday *Highway* series, and there was no person in the entire team more pleased than Harry when I glorified God for saving my soul from the curse of alcohol. He finally commended my witness to an estimated ten million viewers. Now, through the medium of his superb recording, he was again backing my simple word to Orkney, Shetland and Highland listeners. I was greatly honoured, and eventually let the jovial big-hearted Welshman know about it.

The Arts Theatre, Kirkwell, was where Victor and I had our final Rally of the islands tour, well organised by Jimic and company. We were supported by the celebrated 'Men of Orkney' choir. What a blessing it was to hear that brilliant ensemble of gifted voices praise God to the highest!

116

Supper over in the Scott home, I climbed the stairs to my place of rest, where I had communion with God. Then switching the electric blanket off I eased my tired limbs between the warm sheets and lay listening to the wind howling and whistling and shaking the window in its frame.

I wasn't perturbed. On the contrary I was thankful that I had friends like Jimic and Chrisabel, and the hundreds of others, who helped and comforted and strengthened me on my Christian walk. I love each one very much.

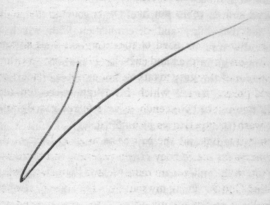

Chapter Twelve

I just could not complete this narrative without saying a word about TBF Thompson, of Garvagh, who started me off on my testimonial trail back in November, 1976.

The admiration of the people of Ulster goes out to him, not alone for the ability and determination with which he meteorically rose to big business success from humble beginnings, but for the high ideals he set himself.

A convert of the Revd. WP Nicholson, whose remarkable ministry I have already referred to, TBF Thompson is firstly a man of God, and I have in ten years of glorious redemption enjoyed the friendship of him and his late wife, Kathleen, and have been blessed and encouraged by their great Christian example.

Mr and Mrs Thompson formed two trusts for the Lord's work – the TBF Thompson Trust and the Mrs TBF Thompson Trust – and these will go on for all time non profit-making in the financial sense as there is no charge for any of the services under the Trusts.

Tom and Kathleen had been keen to provide a holiday home for the aged, people with indifferent health and, perhaps, those feeling forgotten and unwanted. The genial couple, without thought for their own privacy, decided to build a spacious home adjacent to their own summer residence, Rock House, which overlooks the beautiful Portstewart Bay, and from where a wide vista of the west can be seen when the colourful orb of day is sinking to rest behind the Donegal Hills.

Today, Rock House Holiday Home residents, coming for two weeks from the smokey cities and towns and country areas of the Province, find solace and renewed vigour from the clean ocean breezes and, not least, close fellowship with God. The matron and staff do an excellent job, and their home-baking and cooking of real wholesome food is superb.

Under the Mrs TBF Thompson Trust, a pub bought in Garvagh was soon transformed into the full service of God. Known now as *The Corner Stone*, it is in charge of a sincere young Christian couple, Mervyn and Alison Burnside, who work in faith towards the spiritual welfare of the children and youth of the town and district, the Lord blessing their efforts in this important field.

Then Tom and Kathleen, untiring and strong in their love for God, felt that they should expand. After much prayer and discussion a part of the TBF Thompson business premises in Garvagh was selected to become the new complex from which the TBF Thompson Ministries would operate. The facilities available include a large well-equipped and comfortable auditorium where Christian Conferences and functions can be held from time to time.

But sadly, before the renovations were completed, Mrs Thompson suffered an illness and was admitted to hospital. One afternoon I went to the hospital with the hope of seeing the dear lady, but the surgeon was in her ward, so I left a message and came away with the words she spoke to me after I had given my first testimony in Garvagh ringing in my ears. 'It is no secret what God can do. Keep serving Him.'

Two days after my visit Mrs Thompson was called to glory, but before she passed on, a friend said to her: 'God loves you and Christ died for you.' To which Kathleen replied: 'That's all I've got, there is nothing else.'

Mr and Mrs Thompson had jointly founded the TBF Thompson Ministries, and at the memorable opening of the new auditorium Tom had the splendid building dedicated to

119

the glory of God in loving memory of his wonderful partner for thirty-eight happy and unforgettable years and to the furtherance of the Gospel.

Two former moderators of the Presbyterian Church in Ireland, the Very Revd. Dr. William M. Craig, and the Very Revd. Dr. John Girvan, officiated at the ceremony and, fittingly – Mrs AM England – a sister of Mrs Thompson – unveiled the memorial plaque.

There was no mistaking the interest shown by the community at large. The auditorium had a capacity congregation and other parts of the vast complex were used to accommodate the overflow.

I was very impressed with the personal comments of Miss Betty Kelly, Mr Thompson's secretary, on the occasion. She described Mrs Thompson as: 'a lady who did not seek the limelight for herself, but possessed qualities which enabled her in a quiet and practical way to be of help to others. Above all, Mrs Thompson's burning desire was that her loved ones, friends and those of us with whom she came into contact, would come to know the Saviour, as she most certainly did, so that all would one day share in the heavenly Home which God has prepared for his own.'

The TBF Ministries are quite extraordinary. There is available within their precincts Gospel material in the form of literature, sound and video cassettes and 16 mm films, and also cassette players for those folk who are, unfortunately, 'shut in' and unable to enjoy fellowship with friends because of old age or affliction.

In charge of this work on a full-time basis are Vernon Arbuthnot and wife Joy, who show appropriate films in church halls, schools, nursing homes, and private homes. It is proving to be an outstanding witness.

Miss Joan Swann is also engaged in the administration attached to the various activities of the Ministries.

The Ministries, with everything free of charge, also provide transport to take relatives to visit dear ones in hospitals, or to bring comfort in times of bereavement.

As I mentioned, Tom Thompson was a close associate of the late Revd. WP Nicholson, and the last time the great evangelist preached in Northern Ireland was for Tom. Therefore, he felt very privileged when Mrs Nicholson presented him with a master tape of twelve sermons by her late husband which had been recorded over thirty years ago. Tom later arranged for them to be transferred on to cassettes and already there are 12,000 available to be shared with others who wish to hear the preaching of this great evangelist of the past.

TBF Thompson Ministries produced another cassette — *God Loves You* — with the lovely voice of Mildred Rainey singing some of Mrs Thompson's favourite hymns. It has brought sunshine and hope into thousands of homes. I was deeply moved by the special piece — *God loves me* — which was written by Mildred who felt inspired to compose this song on hearing of the last words spoken by Mrs Thompson. This cassette is now being widely used throughout the world for the extension of Christ's Kingdom.

My eldest daughter, Mrs LV McAuley, was affectionately known as Nina. To many folk young and old, and particularly to the members of our large family circle, she was a bright star and counsel. Whatever our troubles were, we went to Nina and always came away enlightened.

It was fifteen years ago that this loving mother of eight children had a mysterious ailment in her right foot which rapidly spread to both legs and cruelly paralysed her. The result was confinement to a wheelchair.

With great courage Nina prayed and entered leading hospitals in Belfast and London and underwent operation after operation in a bid to walk. At all times surgeons and fellow patients acclaimed her the life and soul of the ward.

Behind her never-fading smile, my daughter suffered, yet in the midst of her pain she had concerned thoughts for me and my heavy drink problem.

It was at this time that an extraordinary incident occurred. Once a month Nina attended a Divine Healing meeting in a church hall. She was generally taken there by her husband Victor, but on one occasion he was unable to go, and as a last resort I was asked to oblige.

I agreed wholeheartedly, but was worried about carrying my daughter, for I had little strength through the lack of food. I couldn't eat. Booze was my sole sustenance.

And that physical weakness was my failure in the errand of mercy. I just managed to carry Nina to her wheelchair at the top of the church hall steps when my back gave a loud crack! I fell to the ground writhing in pain and whining like a wounded hare. I was of the opinion that I had fractured my spine!

A big strong clergyman picked me up, and minutes later I found myself – a priority figure at the thoughtful Nina's request, I suspected – sitting in the healing chair in front of a mass of sympathetic disabled people. Then the Revd. Dr James McFarland laid hands on me and prayed for my recovery.

But I had neither faith nor belief in Dr McFarland and his ministry. Two things occupied my fuddled mind – the danger of permanent injury through this new calamity, and the pub two streets away.

I eventually arrived at the pub with my story of woe; I was agonisingly stooped, an awkward stance I was compelled to adopt for months, during which time I visited doctors, masseurs, bone-setters, and 'quack' doctors and tried all kinds of modern and old country and gypsy cures without success.

Miraculously, the back trouble left me on the morning of my conversion and a jubilant Nina rigidly maintained that God had begun to take an interest in my ill-spent life the second Dr McFarland laid hands on me. I heartily agreed.

On a Sunday morning in January, 1987, tragic news reached me of Nina's sudden death. I never realised until then that it was possible to experience the sense of poignancy that welled up in me. I was speechless for hours. The tears just wouldn't stop.

Dear Nina had been a part of me, and was greatly comforted by my sobriety and Christian transformation. She was enthusiastically looking forward to the publication of this book, the writing of which she actually suggested and encouraged.

But we were to find consolation in the words of Revd. David McIlwrath, who conducted the service prior to interment. The young cleric said: 'The only thing that will survive death is Christian character. God's future purposes are a new body. Paul wrote: "Our citizenship is in Heaven. And we eagerly await a Saviour from there, the Lord Jesus Christ, who, by the power that enables Him, will transform our lowly bodies so that they will be like His glorious body." '

'Twill be wonderful to see Nina walking again and rid of the pain and discomfort she endured when down here.

Friday, 24th April, 1987 was a very special time for me and I enjoyed every single second of it. But let me explain from the beginning.

At dawn I was collected by Mr and Mrs Lowry Norris, and courteously chauffeured to Belfast airport, where I got a plane to Birmingham. I was on my way to the 36th Annual Convention of Gideons International in the British Isles. I was to speak after dinner that evening.

Gideons are Christian business and professional men who believe that the Bible is the inspired Word of God, and that its message is relevant to the problems and pressures of the critical days in which we live.

The movement was formed in Wisconsin, USA, in 1899 by three Christian commercial travellers – Samuel Hill, Will Knight and John Nicholson.

John maintained a life-long habit of reading a portion of the Bible every day, the outcome of a promise made at the age of thirteen to his dying mother. This was a vital factor in the commencement of Gideons, whose initial purpose was simply to provide Christian fellowship amongst business men.

In 1903 an American Gideon visiting England discovered that the Commercial Travellers Christian Association were placing Bibles in hotels. He took the idea back with him to America and in 1908 Gideons also began distributing Bibles, not only to hotels, but other important public centres such as schools, hospitals, prisons and senior citizens' homes.

It was not until towards the end of 1949 that the Gideon ministry was officially launched in the British Isles, and the work expanded rapidly. Today there are more than two hundred and thirty-five branches around the country, handing out almost one million Bibles and Testaments annually.

I can say with joy in my heart that the school children – Catholic and Protestant – of the trouble-torn areas of Northern Ireland have been the recipients of Gideon New Testaments and look upon the magnanimous gesture with gratitude and affection.

With the printing of the various Gideon Scriptural books, enormous expense is involved and this is met through members' annual subscriptions and public contributions.

The work is interdenominational as well as universal. Members distribute the Word of God in over one hundred and thirty countries at the phenomenal rate of *two million* copies every month.

This world-wide service is really an extended arm of the church, for all Gideons are members in good standing of local churches, and they meet together for Christian service and witness and, apart from providing Bibles, share the joy of their faith in Christ by personal testimony.

My readers are already aware that a Gideon New Testament helped to direct me into God's family, so in my address I was all geared up to express grateful thanks to the men who placed the Good Book on the locker beside my hospital bed.

Trauma and tragedy frequently result in time spent in hospital. Admission more often than not produces anxiety and fear. At such times patients look for reassurance, comfort and encouragement. The Gideons have found that the true source of such help is found in Jesus, who reveals Himself in the Bible. I can endorse this fully with my personal experience.

I find interest in the familiar small lapel badge worn by Gideons throughout the world, which illustrates the message of the Book of Judges, chapters six and seven. The emblem incorporates the trumpet (gold circle) with the pitcher (white) and the flame of the torch (red). In the story of Gideon, God reduced an army of 32,000 men to a small dedicated band of three hundred who were victorious in battle against a massive army.

The convention was held in the Metropole Hotel, Birmingham. My room number was 1072, and that was only half-way along the second floor! I think it was six floors I observed on the lift indicator, so it was little wonder the Irish country boy got lost three times and was scared out of his wits.

But I must say that the hundreds of people around me from every corner of Britain were exceptionally kind and helpful, and I could never really describe the wonderful liberty God gave me when speaking to them in the vast auditorium.

Following the national president's epilogue, on making my way from the platform, a farmer from Suffolk approached me and said: 'My sons and I were anticipating a barley crop this year, but through your testimony the Lord has spoken to me and there will be no barley grown while I'm around.'

Well, looking at the farmer's decision logically, less barley means less whiskey, so my journey to Birmingham had not been in vain from that point of view.

Over the years I have received many letters from readers of my newspaper page *People and Places* in different parts of the world, particularly America and Canada. The correspondents had, perhaps, found special interest, nostalgia or traced long-lost relatives or friends through something I had written. Quite a number extended invitations to visit them should I ever be their way.

On 2nd May, 1987 I arrived in Toronto, Canada, to look up several of those kind people and broaden the horizons of my page by doing articles on them. At the same time, and more important, I was to participate in the Lord's work.

In one of the early chapters I told you of the butterflies that invaded my stomach prior to my first testimony commitment. Believe me they were nothing in comparison to the three nests of crawling creatures that erupted in my abdominal system the morning I was to audition for the *100 Huntley Street* television programme which is seen the length and breadth of Canada, and on eighteen independent stations in the United States, and is available to more than 1,000 cable outlets.

Billy Graham, Arthur Blessitt, Pat Boone, Dale Evans Rogers, our own Malcolm Muggeridge, Chuck Colson, Hal Lindsay, author of *The Late Great Planet Earth*, and other world-famous men and women too numerous to mention have appeared on *100 Huntley Street*, so as I strolled into the large red-bricked building in downtown Toronto, from where the programme goes out daily. In rhythmic addition to the mad dance of the butterflies my two knees were knocking and I wished and wished that I was on my way out.

It was TBF Thompson who said after my first testimony in his Irish mission hall: 'God has plans for you, Speedy.'

Well, begorra, what was He going to do with me in the immensity of this set-up?

And the pretty receptionist didn't alleviate the performance of butterflies and knocking knees in any way when she found my North Irish semi-Scottish brogue difficult to understand. How about the millions of viewers for whom I was supposed to be potential material? Och, dear, but oul' Ireland seemed far, far, far, away.

But in the next half-hour a wee word of prayer, the warmth of Ralph Bradley, the guest co-ordinator, and two strong coffees, had calmed me down considerably. After chatting with Ralph for a while it was as if we had known each other for a lifetime.

Then the guest co-ordinator sparked off our first argument. He stressed that his surname, Bradley, was of English origin, his grandfather having been born in London. I countered strongly and patriotically by insisting that the name Bradley had its roots in Ireland, and that my new-found friend's forebears, like so many others, emigrated to London at one time.

And 'shure an' begorra' where else could young Ralph have got that radiant smile and racy patter from, but the oul' green sod nestlin' in the North Atlantic?

My audition over and, thankfully, successful, I was contracted to appear and speak on the *100 Huntley Street* series of 20th May – a big assignment for the oul' Irish country scribe, but I looked forward to the challenge with confidence knowing that God was my guide and inspiration.

Ralph introduced me to the Revd. Jack Hunka, host for the television programme *Nasha Nadia* which reaches tens of thousands of Ukrainians with the gospel message. He is also responsible for weekly telecasts in French, Italian, German, Greek, Arabic, Finnish, Romanian, and *Signs of the Times* for the deaf and dumb. But this busy man confesses that his department is just scratching the surface of the matter, for in Toronto alone there are one hundred and twenty-two different languages spoken.

The Revd. David Mainse, head of Crossroad Christian Communications, which he formed in 1962, is host for the *100 Huntley Street* programme. With his striking personality, rich turn of phrase, and knowledge of the Scriptures, he is ready-made for the job.

When David began to broadcast a short programme in 1962 on a Northern Ontario television station, neither he nor anyone else could ever have imagined the impact his ministry was going to have on Canada, and, indeed, the United States.

Some worldly people were of the opinion that David Mainse was a fabulously wealthy man, like a number of evangelicals in the neighbouring US are supposed to be. While guesting on a chat-show on CBC, Canada's Government-owned network, David was suddenly attacked and accused of paying himself a huge salary and accepting lavish corporation perks, like a big posh house, a Jag and a private plane.

But the abrupt interviewer knew he had made a mistake when his subject calmly declared that he lived in a modest apartment, drove a five-year-old car, and earned less than the camera man facing him. And he had a recent tax return to prove the authenticity of his non-hesitant reply.

I find Canada a place of extreme pressure and tension principally because of its agricultural and industrial activities. It brings prosperity to those who want to work, and I am pleased to say that the Irish folk, northern and southern, I met here have not missed out on the opportunity the vast country has to offer.

Because of the aforementioned pressure and tension the earlier Canadian Governments realised that there was a definite need for people to relax. That resulted in the forming of great National Parks. They are prominent throughout the

128

land and contain everything natural at its best. And everyone is encouraged to take advantage of them during their leisure moments.

But even with those amenities, I doubt if I could settle down permanently admist the hustle and bustle and different cultures of a Canadian or American city. Yesterday morning I sat in the centre of Toronto and in two hours almost every nationality in the world must have walked past me. I could see then the authority of telecaster Jack Hunka when he referred to the one hundred and twenty-two languages spoken locally, and understood perfectly the mammoth task that faces him in the presentation of the Gospel.

Few Ulstermen and women holidaying in Canada fail to visit an Eaton's Store. Apart from purchasing, it is a kind of pilgrimage, for Timothy Eaton, the founder of the gigantic chain, was the youngest of a family of nine children who lived on a small farm outside Ballymena, County Antrim.

Born over one hundred and thirty years ago, Timothy left school at the age of thirteen and apprenticed himself to the drapery and grocery trades in a little shop in Portglenone, County Antrim, which still stands. In fact, I was in it recently.

Young Timothy didn't complete his apprenticeship there, for sometimes he worked from 5 am till midnight before crawling into his bed beneath a counter in the shop.

With a few pounds in his pocket he went to Canada and lived in Kirkton, Ontario. Two years later he joined his brother James in the operation of a general store in St Mary's, Ontario.

In December 1869 Timothy opened a shop in Toronto, and astonished fellow merchants by declaring that if a customer didn't like what he or she had bought in the store, they could return it and get their money back. He also laid down another couple of basics that were pretty revolutionary for their time. A good sound church-goer, he marked goods

129

with a fixed price so there would be no haggling. And he sold everything for cash.

The result of Timothy Eaton's efforts are the big stores in Canadian cities today employing some seventy thousand people. And they honour the founder's dying rule – no tobacco, no alcoholic beverages for sale.

With that history of a fellow Ulsterman's stupendous success firmly planted in my mind from boyhood, I went to Eaton's Toronto store in search of a nice blue shirt for my forthcoming telly appearance.

A well-mannered, well-dressed, respectable young man soon made me a satisfied customer. In the courtesy and power of his salesmanship I could see the thrift and zeal of Timothy Eaton.

Before leaving I said to the young man, and not without expanded chest: 'Are you aware that your late boss, Timothy Eaton, was an Ulsterman?'

The young man eyed me up and down and then gently rubbing his smooth chin murmured: 'What is an Ulsterman, sir?'

My stay in Toronto is full of interest and the people I meet are very friendly, but I am now threescore-and-ten plus, and a wee bit tired of wandering. A longing for the emerald isle, the place of my birth, possesses me continually. I thank God again for His great love and mercy towards me, and I will acclaim Him in every way possible as I live in the evening of this life, awaiting the next at His right hand. Amen!